FORMATTING
E-BOOKS
FOR WRITERS

SUSAN K. STEWART

PG A PRACTICAL GUIDE

Formatting e-Books for Writers

by Susan K. Stewart

Published by

Practical Inspirations

P. O. Box 561

Luling, TX 78648

www.practicalinspirations.com

Editor: Jeanne Leach

There are no affiliate links in this book.

Publishing and Design Services: MelindaMartin.me

ISBN: 978-0-9767394-2-5

Library of Congress Control Number: 2016936445

Updated March 2018

10 9 8 7 6 5 4 3

ENDORSEMENTS

"So much wonderful information!"

Linda W. Yezak, Writer/Editor
Circle-Bar Ranch Series
Give the Lady a Ride
The Final Ride

"A comprehensive, well-written and best of all, VERY easy to understand book that delivers on its promises to guide authors who have wanted to tip-toe in the waters of learning to publish e-books on their own."

Mary Aucoin Kaarto
Author, Speaker and Encourager
HOPE for the LAID OFF — Devotionals
HELP for the LAID OFF

"Susan's insights are practical. I'm so grateful she has compiled them into a book. I could really apply this RIGHT NOW."

Nicolas Nelson
Wordsmith Writing Coaches

"After taking the class, I think the book does an excellent job of bringing together all the finer details of formatting e-books. I feel this book is comprehensive enough to give even a newbie like me, a good big-picture of what formatting eBooks is about as well as an excellent guide as to how to do it."

Sharon Ford

Freelance Proofread/Copyeditor

"Susan Stewart has written an excellent guide to self-publishing e-books. Susan formatted the guide in a logical fashion with easy-to-understand steps to follow for each part of the process. Anyone who chooses to self-publish should have *Formatting e-Books for Writers* … they'll find the suggestions enable them to publish a professional book."

Deb Haggerty

Elk Lake Publishing, Inc.

CONTENTS

Preface.. ix
Acknowledgements... xiii

CHAPTER ONE
INTRODUCTION TO E-BOOKS 1

Micro-history...2
Difference between e-books and print books............................4
File formats...7
E-book readers...8
Industry changes..9

CHAPTER TWO
STEPS TO A GOOD E-BOOK... 13

Step one—Write a good book..14
Step two—Edit a good book..16
Step three—Create a great cover 17
Step four—Consider the reader..18

CHAPTER THREE
DECISIONS 23

Technical details..25
Who is doing the work? 26
Distribution channels...26
Directly from Amazon, Apple App Store, etc. 27

Third Party Distributors (Aggregators) 29
Your Website..29
In Person..30
Sidebars, pull quotes, and other extras.....................32
Exclusivity 32
Sharing 33
Which comes first: print or e-book? 36

CHAPTER FOUR
AMAZON PUBLISHING SERVICES

.... 41

CHAPTER FIVE
WHILE YOU WRITE

.... 49

Title..50
Description 51
Categories 52
Keywords 53
Cover..53
Marketing...55
Set up accounts..56
Price..58
Website/blog...58

CHAPTER SIX
OTHER PRE-PUBLICATION CONSIDERATIONS

.... 61

Pricing 61
Marketing...65
Prerelease campaign 71

CHAPTER SEVEN
THE FOUNDATION

....75

CHAPTER EIGHT
BASIC STEPS TO FORMATTING 87

    Let's begin 88
    Cleaning up 90
    Hidden Format Code 95
    Basic starting steps 96
    Change Fonts 96
    Sidebars 97

CHAPTER NINE
NEXT FORMATTING STEPS 103

    Inserting page breaks 103
    Now the small details 105
    Paragraphs 106
    Preparing the table of contents 107
    Building the table of contents 109

CHAPTER TEN
FINAL FORMATTING DETAILS 115

    Front matter 115
    Footnotes 116
    Website URLs 117

CHAPTER ELEVEN
GRAPHICS, TEXT BOXES, COVERS 121

    Images 121
    Text Boxes 124
    Tables 126
    Text with Graphics 127
    File Storage 127
    Inserting images 128
    Fixed-layout books 130
    Covers 130
    One Small Detail 132

CHAPTER TWELVE
PUBLISHING YOUR E-BOOK **135**

File type 136
Prepare the HTML file 137
Conversion step one—HTML...................................138
Conversion step two—Graphic files.........................139
File Upload 141
Uploading your book 142
Correcting problems 148
Problems after publishing..150

CHAPTER THIRTEEN
TROUBLESHOOTING **153**

Appendix 1: Formatting Checklist............................159
Appendix 2: E-Publishing Terms 161
Appendix 3: Set Up Kindle Direct Publishing
              (KDP) Account 165
Appendix 4: Formatting PDF E-Books.....................167
Appendix 5: Changes For Epub Files........................177
Appendix 6: Metadata And Keywords 180
Appendix 7: Print Books 184
Appendix 8: Resources 186
Appendix 9: Chapter Resource Links 198

About the Author 209
Connect with Susan 211

PREFACE

I'm a hands-on control freak. Not only do I want to learn things, but I also want to know exactly what is happening to my projects. When something goes wrong, I want to know why and how to fix it. So I decided to tackle creating my own e-books.

It began with a simple PDF. At the time, word processors didn't easily convert to or export to PDF files. It required knowing how to use the Adobe products. Well, at least, being able to muddle through the products. (That's me, a muddler.) The PDF e-book looked exactly like my print book and sold well. At the time, there were so many things I didn't know and learned through "hard knocks."

A few years later, I decided my next book should be a Kindle book. Actually it was easier than the PDF book. Of course, I needed to work through problems as they cropped up. Using the many resources available, I learned an easier way. After my Kindle started selling, I went onto other e-bookstores as well, which meant learning to create an EPUB file also.

I've translated what I learned to help others by converting their products to various e-book files. As I've converted files for others, I found many writers would like to at least know the process, how to make it easier for another to make the conversion for them, and possibly go DIY in the future.

This led to online classes teaching both what e-publishing is and how to easily create and prepare a Word document for conversion to any of the e-book formats. Like my conversion clients, often those who take the class aren't interested in actually doing the conversion themselves. Instead, they only want to know the process.

This is the next step in my journey with e-publishing—a book to help you learn the steps of the process.

Before we get started, here are a few things to know this book. What it is not:

- A how-to-write book. While a couple of chapters do help you create the best possible product, I assume you at least have a draft manuscript.

- A web design process. There are a number of wonderful resources for creating your webpage, but I'm not the expert in design.

- A business book. There is a chapter on marketing ideas, but I'm a writer, not a business consultant. I know what has worked for me, which I will share.

What you will find:

- Details of formatting a manuscript into a downloadable e-product.

- Steps to publishing a Kindle product.

- This 2018 edition includes the updated information about publishing at Kindle Direct Publishing.

At the end of each chapter, I've included some steps to help you move forward, cleverly called "Move Forward." It's very easy to read a how-to book, put the book down, and not do anything. I write from experience; I've done it. I hope these assignments will help you get your book ready for publication. That's my goal.

Some of us like to jump right in with the task at hand. I urge everyone to read the preliminary chapters. The actual formatting instructions begin in Chapter 8. During breaks from preparing the manuscript, go back to the first four chapters for information about pricing, marketing, and other details for a professional and first-class Kindle book.

I've also included checklist for the people who like list. If you would like to print it, here's a link http://bit.ly/format_checklist.

All the resource links are also listed at my website http://practicalinspirations.com/format_resources/.

It's my hope you will find the instructions in this book helpful as you prepare to publish your e-book.

Susan K. Stewart
January 2018

For e-book hints and up-to-date information, subscribe to

Practical Inspirations News
http://eepurl.com/9vdS5

ACKNOWLEDGEMENTS

Although my name is on the front of the book, I didn't do this alone. So many people have helped in so many different ways. Some were hands-on and others were encouragers.

My husband, Bob, is my head cheerleader. He listens as I whine, offers suggestions that are usually spot-on, and tolerates socks left in the dryer. This is a few of the many reason I love him.

Karen Koch is a terrific editor and ably edited the original manuscript. Editor and friend Jeanne Leach took on the task for this edition. I appreciate both of these ladies' keen eye and help making this a quality product.

Melinda Martin of MartinPublishingServices.com is not just a creative and talented designer. She is also a friend who has been a source of inspiration and blessing. Her work on the design of this edition has been extraordinary.

The WordGirls know what it's like to write a book. This group of ladies prays, encourages, and offers wonderful suggestions. I'm thankful for each one of them.

Beta readers have an important role. These wonderful people are the frontlines in ensuring that you have a book that is readable and useful to you.

Sharon Ford
Deb Haggerty
Diane Hurst
Mary Kaarto
Linda Yezak

Some wonderful people contributed to my Indiegogo crowdfund effort. Their generosity helped me to get this book to market without going into debt.

Carolyn Banks
Janice Green
Nicolas Nelson, Wordsmith Writing Coaches
Carol Peters
Kristen Stieffel, Writer • Editor • Mentor
Tame the Beasties
John Vonhof, Writers & Authors on Fire
Janine Williams

Glory to God. He arranged a divine appointment that pushed me in the way He wanted me to go. It is God's generous gift gives me the ability to teach others through writing. God gave His Son Jesus to clean my dirty heart of the evil and the sin found there.

CHAPTER ONE

INTRODUCTION TO E-BOOKS

According to American Publishers Association's (APA) latest numbers, e-book sales are declining, down by 24.9 per cent. The same report shows a decline in hardback sales, but an increase in paperback sales.[1] According to Forbes magazine, these numbers only include APA members. As Mark Coker of Smashwords points out, these numbers are based on dollar sales. He says, "Since e-books are priced significantly lower than print books, the unit percentage (or percentage of words read in e-book format) is much higher."[2]

I'll be honest; I still like to curl up with print editions. And I'm certainly not taking my e-reader into the bathtub for a long, hot soak. My iPad is full of books and documents, though, for easy transporting when I travel. I even have a few books on my iPhone so I don't have to read years-old magazines while waiting somewhere (even in line at the grocery store).

Not only has e-publishing changed the book industry, but also many newspapers and magazines are offering their products in electronic media as well as print versions. In fact, many magazines are only offering digital versions. *Newsweek* suspended print editions for nearly two years due to revenue loss. E-textbooks for college, even some high schools, are a growing trend. The *Los Angeles Times*, however, reported in February 2016 that more than 90% of students prefer print books.[3] In 2013, Scribd launched Netflix-like subscription service for e-books. For a monthly fee, subscribers can read as many e-books as they wish. Soon Amazon followed suit with Kindle Unlimited. Libraries are also loaning e-books.

Writers can no longer ignore e-publishing. While I don't think print books will ever completely go away, the future looks to be electronic. Some titles, which have been backlisted[4] by the publisher, are seeing new life through self-publishing by the author. Those of us who are publishing through a traditional publishing company will probably have the e-book versions handled by the publishing company along with print. Be sure to check the contract. If e-versions are included in the contract, find out the details and options. I'm not a lawyer or agent, so I advise getting help.

Micro-history

In the beginning there was only one way to read anything electronic—on a computer. At first, there was a lot of confusion among the various computer operating systems. Early in this history, most computers were still operating in DOS (disk operating system); certainly not a pretty way to use a computer.

Apple computers were the first to have a graphic user interface (GUI–pronounced "gooey"). Not long after, Microsoft created Windows. Windows systems (or now lovingly known as the PC) wouldn't read something from a Mac, and Mac had an aversion to anything PC.

Computer geniuses somewhere, probably in the dark, solved the problem by creating file formats each system liked: Rich Text Format (RTF) and Portable Document Format (PDF). But the problem of having to sit at a computer and read still existed. The other alternative was to print out the document, which in the case of a book could be hundreds of pages. Sometimes printing the entire book cost more than just buying the paperback. In these early days, traditional publishers had no worries about e-books taking over the industry.

Project Gutenberg was one of the first to take advantage of the electronic publishing format. In 1971, Michael Hart developed the idea of putting public domain books and documents in electronic format for all to have. He began by using the most basic form readable by all types of computers, ASCII text. Over the years, Project Gutenberg has expanded to include all e-reader types. The goal of Project Gutenberg still is to have all public domain books available to the general public.

Then Sony came up with a better idea—the e-reader named the Data Discman. This device used compact discs (CDs) to store the book. At the time, 1992 (pre-historic in technology time), most of the books were technical manuals. In 2006, Sony produced the first e-reader to download material directly to the device. A year later Amazon released the Kindle, and as the trite saying goes, "The rest is history." Kindle now dominates the market. Industry insiders believe, however, increased tablet sales and the introduction of iBooks Store on all Apple devices may change Kindle's domination.[5]

In ancient electronic times, five or six years ago, many of us (I do include myself) didn't think e-books would become a revolution. I didn't own my first e-reader until 2010, though I published an e-book in 2005.

After the introduction of the Sony e-reader and Kindle, several other companies created their own version. Several are still file specific, reading only their brand's files. Most e-reader brands, except Apple's iBooks, now have an application so their e-products can be read on multiple devices. Books purchased through the iBooks Store are only available for Apple devices.

Readers are expecting more from all books. I'm seeing more books, especially nonfiction including CDs with extra content and/or exclusive online content. I believe this is an attempt to make print books more attractive to those who prefer e-books. What is it about e-books that make them so appealing?

Difference between e-books and print books

While most of us think the difference between an e-book and a print book is the method of reading, there really is more to it.

- Instant Availability. In the internet age and, quite honestly, in the culture of instant gratification, having the product instantly available is a big plus.

- Storage. E-readers can store hundreds and thousands of books, magazines, and other documents. This type of storage capability saves shelf space and the need for a place to put those shelves. I like the idea of not weighing down my suitcase with my various reading materials. Because e-books can also be stored on a smartphone, reading material is readily available. Kindle products even sync between devices, so it isn't necessary to "thumb" through the pages to find your place.

- Flexibility. The reader can choose the size and sometimes the style of text. This makes e-books attractive for readers who may have vision disabilities. The newer e-readers have the capability to dim or brighten the background for reading in the dark or in bright sunlight. Most devices also have voice capabilities, which will read the book aloud.

- Bookmarks and Notes. Placing bookmarks, highlighting text, and making notes are easy in e-books. No pencils or pens are required. Kindle books can show the passages other readers have highlighted.

- Price. Price is not as much a positive factor as it was even a year ago. Some e-books are now priced nearly the same as print. Whether publishers are doing this to increase print sales or increase profit is not known, but e-books for the most part are cheaper than print books. In addition, the price of e-readers is coming down.

- Interactivity. As devices become more sophisticated, the ability to add video and audio, along with sharing notes with other readers, makes e-books more attractive. Technology is now moving forward with 3D objects in e-books, allowing the reader to rotate objects or scenes. Younger readers are coming to expect such interactivity. With the ability to include links within the text and in the endnotes, it's easy to find more information while reading. Many writers also include Facebook and Twitter links so readers can share what they have read with friends.

- Multimedia Capability. Newer devices are capable of linking to the internet, showing videos, and displaying animation.

- Environmentally Sound. This is an important factor to some readers. E-books don't use paper or fuel for shipping the books.

- Accessibility to International Markets. In the print-only days, a publisher or agent negotiated terms with international distributors to produce a book overseas. Because an e-book is generally delivered via the internet, authors can now immediately have an international distribution.

File formats

There is no one standard e-book format. Wikipedia lists about thirty different e-book formats. A lot of documents can be transferred and read on most e-readers. The market has shuffled down to four popular formats.

- PDF. This format has been used for years, even before e-readers. It is a standard format useable on both Windows and Mac platforms. PDF take little effort to make and is easy to download from websites. The drawbacks are readers may need to manually transfer the file to their e-reader, and these files are not as flexible in e-readers. Occasionally, because the formatting may not work, a PDF file will not look good on an e-reader.

- EPUB. The iBook, Nook, and Kobo are among the e-readers that use EPUB format. It has a different conversion method than PDFs and Kindle books. On the plus side, more devices can read an EPUB document. Only the Kindle does not. The newest EPUB format, EPUB 3, allows interactive features through special coding.

- MOBI. Many devices can read MOBI files, including the Kindle. It is the foundation file for Kindle's AZW. It is not graphic friendly, however. A standard MOBI doesn't allow for much interaction.

- AZW. Amazon developed its own file format and it is used exclusively on the Kindle. There are variations on the AZW file format, which are used for various e-book types and the Kindle reader. (AZW may mean "Amazon Word.")

Some people believe, even with just four popular formats, there are too many. Before cross-platform apps became available, this was a problem because each format required a specific device, which is not much of a problem now.

E-book readers

By far the most well-known e-reader is Amazon's Kindle. That doesn't particularly mean that all Kindle formatted e-books are being read on Amazon's e-readers. Amazon has created apps for nearly every mobile device, plus both Windows and Mac operating systems. So has Nook. Both of these companies make it possible to purchase products even without their device. Apple, however, hasn't created cross-platform apps for iBooks. That doesn't mean that e-books formatted for the iBook store can only be read on an Apple device, however. iBooks are EPUB files and can be made available to other devices through various distribution companies.

In addition to Kindle, Nook, and iBooks, Kobo has several devices as well as apps for most mobile devices. Sony sold their US e-book market to Kobo.

The point is the specific e-reader is now a matter of convenience and preference. I read all of my e-books on my iPad. I do have a Kindle I use to test viewing when creating my own e-books.

Industry changes

Books, print and electronic, can now be produced faster and are available to a broader market. My Kindle products are sold around the world. Each month I have sales from other countries.

The publishing process has changed because of e-books. A majority of e-books are self-published. This fact reflects a change in the publishing world. No longer are the Big 5 publishing companies in charge of what will be available to the reading public. Traditional publishers are no longer the sole go-between with the writer and the audience or the sole route to market.

E-books have changed the production flow for traditional publishers, as well. From creation to consumption, time is cut in half from traditional print channels.

In a talk to the California Writers Club in 2013, Mark Coker listed more advantages of e-publishing:

- Faster time to market.
- Lower expenses.
- Better distribution to the global market.
- Never out of print.
- Lower prices to consumer.
- Earn more per book.[6]

End Notes

1. "Publishers Sales Down at the Start of 2016, eBooks Decline," Association of American Publishers, June 27, 2016, http:// newsroom.publishers.org/publishers-sales-down-at-the-start- of-2016-ebooks-decline/ accessed March 20, 2017.

2. Coker, Mark, "E-book workshop: E-books and the future of publishing," presented at California Writers Club, Sacramento, CA, September 29, 2012, slides 12, 14, http:// bit.ly/2nKsUoN, accessed March 20, 2017.

3. "92% of college students prefer print books to e-books, study finds," *Los Angeles Times*, February 8, 2016, http://lat. ms/2k4vC8V, accessed March 20, 2017.

4. Backlist is the books that publishers keep in print over several years, as opposed to newly released titles. The term backlist is used because these books are listed in the back of a publishers' catalog.

5. Greenfield, Jeremy, 2014, "Will Apples new iOS8 help it take on Amazon's Kindle dominance," *Forbes*, https:// www.forbes.com/sites/jeremygreenfield/2014/09/17/ will-apples-new-ios-8-help-it-take-on-amazons-kindle- dominance/#6da9b1b11c8e, accessed December 17, 2015

6. Coker, Mark, 2012, "E-book workshop: E-books and the future of publishing," presented at California Writers Club

Sacramento, CA, September 29, 2012, slides 23, http://bit.ly/2nKsUoN, accessed March 20, 2017.

CHAPTER TWO

STEPS TO A GOOD E-BOOK

Most e-books are self-published. Even well-known authors are doing very well self-publishing. But there's still a public perception that self-published books are "bad." Each person has a definition of "bad": poor writing, poor layout, bad cover, or poorly edited. This myth may have been curated by some traditional publishers.

David Gaughran points out in his book *Let's Get Digital, How to Self-Publish, and Why You Should*[1] that traditional publishers think readers want them to curate reading selections based on their expertise. Mr. Gaughran goes on to say, "The average reader rarely knows or cares who published a book." Readers do care, however, about a quality product. Even a free e-book needs to be a quality product.

I agree with Pamela Fagan Hutchinson. In her book *What Kind of Loser Indie Publishes,*[2] she has titled a chapter "Make It Look Easy {Publishing is easy. Good books are hard}." I certainly agree with her assessment. Since the advent of desktop publishing, it seems everyone with a computer has published a document called a book; few were *good* books. Before we even get to the point of formatting, I must mention a few things that need to be done to produce a good e-book.

Step one—Write a good book

For most of us writing a good book sounds like a no-brainer. After all, many of us have written and published multiple articles and books. Have you seen those ads for "Write an E-book in an Hour"? Have you seen those e-books?

Some writers can hammer out an article or even a chapter or two in an hour. Actually I can do a 1,500-word article in about an hour. But that's just typing words to computer file, not research or re-writing, and certainly not publishable material.

An increasingly popular method of writing a book is by blogging the book. When done correctly, a good product can be the result. Sadly some bloggers think they can take a bunch of blog posts and string them together, and violà, an e-book. I just finished reading one of those. The writer didn't bother to re-read the material. Not everything fit with the subject of the book and there was a lot of duplication. While I did glean a few tidbits of information, I'm glad I didn't pay for the book.[3]

Let's take a moment and look at the differences between a chapter in a book and a blog post.

- Length. I've written this chapter as blog posts. Please note the plural here. Each one of the steps is a separate blog post of 150 to 300 words.

- Style of writing. The writing in this book is a little more formal than what I use on my blog. In a blog post I may use fragmented sentence, more slang, and generally a less formal tone. Why? Sometimes a blog post becomes a conversation and we are far less formal in a conversation.

- Less detail. A blog post often has less technical detail. It's more of a summary.

Granted, not everyone writes a blog post the way I do. Some bloggers would use this chapter as one post. However, many readers may quit reading. It's possible to use blog posts for the foundation of a book. But the writer still has work to do.
It's far too easy to be tempted to hack out something, then toss it up on Amazon for 99 cents, and simply wait for the money to roll in. Even for well-established writers, the promise of fast publication is tempting.

We all want a good product. To have it, we need to start with the basics of solid writing. The first basic point is to follow all the rules of writing we've all learned over the years.

Even when planning to convert a print book already in publication, go back to basics. Re-read the manuscript.

- Is there new information that changes a nonfiction book?

- Did some errors slip through? My most recent book was edited by three different editors. When I went through it before converting it to Kindle, I was amazed at the number of little mistakes I found.

- Can anything be written better? I'm sure we can all find a sentence that can be improved.

Step two—Edit a good book

As professional writers, we understand the need for good editing to create an excellent product. I'm glad to be reading that more self-published writers are emphasizing the need for professional editing. Our books' success depends on it. David Gaughran tells us two times that we'll regret not having our manuscripts professionally edited.

It's far too easy to think we can edit our own material. Of course, we need to be the first editor. But we also need different eyes on our writing. Even when I'm writing a short paragraph for a website, I try to have someone else look at it before I send it out for primetime.

Your spouse, your parent, and your friend who teaches English literature are not professional editors. My husband is my first reader, but he's not an editor. He does have an eye for what doesn't work. I would probably call him my "alpha reader." Yes, he gets it before a beta reader. I repeat, he is not my editor. A friend or relative may or may not know good grammar and

English writing rules. But this person will probably be afraid to give an unbiased (read negative) comment.

A writer's critique group can help work out some of the tricky chapters. But don't let the editing stop there. Hire a professional. The same is true of beta readers. Wikipedia defines beta reader as a non-professional. Beta readers are usually people who love to read and are willing to give feedback to writers. An editor may be among the beta readers, but beta reading is not the same as editing.

I know some may be thinking, "I can't afford it." We can't not afford it. In *What Kind of Loser Indie Publishes*, Pamela Fagan Hutchins gives this advice, "Can't afford an editor? Sell your car. Try crowdfunding. Barter services. Otherwise, wait until you have the money, or go the traditional route." Editing may not be as expensive as it sounds. For my last book, a magazine editor was so interested in the project she was willing to edit in exchange for a set number of copies of the print edition. Whatever it takes, make arrangements to have a professional edit the manuscript.

Step three—Create a great cover

Too often writers think the cover doesn't matter as much for an e-book. Not true. As much care should be given to the cover of an e-book as a print book. David Gaughran says, "A bad cover can sink a book."[4]

An e-book doesn't sit on a bookshelf with hundreds of other

books. But it does sit on a virtual shelf with thousands of other e-books. Remember so many other things on the page grab the online shoppers' attention. Even on a website, the cover needs to be attractive and capture attention. No stock e-book covers please.

In most cases the same cover for a print edition can be used for an e-book. If a print version is not being published, still give deliberate thought to the cover.

A back cover isn't needed for an e-book. Where are all the nice things people have to say about the book? The primary place is in the review section of the online book store and on a review page on your website. Three or four of these reviews and endorsements may be added to the back pages. (Honestly, when I get a book with dozens of pages of compliments, I skip those pages and move right on to the story, especially for a novel. With nonfiction, I look for names I recognize and may or may not read the review.)

Step four—Consider the reader

As writers we know we need to be aware of our audience. This idea, though, is a little different for e-publishing. Our e-books are going to a different medium, a different reading experience. Our audience will have different needs other than just the content. And many readers of an e-book still have print book expectations.

Jonathan Wondrusch says in *The E-Book Creation Explorer's*

Guide,[5] "Every single decision made when creating an e-book plays into the experience that the reader will have."

Remember the reader may be using a computer or a phone to read. Younger readers tend to expect interactive material. Maybe the content requires tables and graphs, which are handled differently in electronic format than print format. With an e-book, the audience may now expect color. Children's books may be greatly enhanced with audio included.

Considering the audience now requires thinking beyond the words on the "page."

Move Forward

Check each of the four steps for your book.

☐ Write a good book. Of course, you've already started this step.

☐ Begin to look for an editor. (See the Resource section)

☐ Begin looking at images for cover ideas. (See the Resource section)

☐ Write a profile of your reader. Likes? Dislikes? Occupation? Hobbies? Just as you might make a character profile, get to know your reader so you can provide a good reading experience.

End Notes

1. Gaughran, David, 2011, *Let's Get Digital: How to Self-Publish and Why You Should*, July 2011, Arriba Arriba Books. A free PDF of the first version of this book is available at http://davidgaughran.wordpress.com/lets-get-digital/

2. Hutchinson, Pamela Fagen, *What Kind of Loser Indie Publishes*, 2013, Skipjack Publishing

3. For information about the right way to blog a book see Nina Amir's book *How to Blog a Book.*

4. Gaughran, David, *Let's Get Digital*

5. Wondrusch, Jonathan, *E-Book Creation Explorer's Guide*, 2010, ByBloggers. No longer available.

CHAPTER THREE

DECISIONS

It's not too early to begin thinking about such things as price, marketing, cover, title, and other e-publishing decisions. Not all of these decisions need to be made immediately. When we start making these decisions early, while writing or formatting our e-book, we won't feel rushed at the end. Aren't those last minute decisions the ones we seem to regret most?

Some questions to think about now:

1. Are you comfortable with a few technical details? (Don't run away; it's easy to learn.)

    While you won't really be digging into the depths of the technical aspects of your e-book, you do need to know a few technical details. You may even want to add certain programming code to have your e-product look and behave exactly as you wish.

2. Are you comfortable working with graphics?

You may not need to actually create graphics for your book although you may need to handle them within the body of your e-book (some of those technical details in question 1 above). Don't think you must be a graphic artist to create and format your e-book. But you shouldn't be uncomfortable with the process either.

3. Do you want to sell your e-product on your website or at events?

   This is a decision you need to make early in the process. It determines some of the file formats you'll need and any extra time you'll require for marketing.

4. Do you want people to be able to share your e-book?

   Believe it or not, writers grapple with this decision. Of course, there are differing opinions. You may want to read those opinions while you're writing your book. (More information about digital rights management [DRM] can be found later in this chapter.)

5. Do you plan to give your book away or offer it free during special promos?

   If this is part of your marketing plan (You are working on your marketing plan, right?), this decision will determine file formats as well as where you sell your product.

6. Will you have a print edition of your book?

This decision may determine where you publish, how you format, and how you distribute and market.

Technical details

As late as 2010, formatting of some e-books required knowledge of various programming languages. In the early days, few e-books even had clickable table of contents because extra programming skills were required. Amazon's Kindle revolutionized e-book publishing not just with the e-reader for everyone, but also with the ease of publishing an e-book. Through Kindle Direct Publishing (KDP), a Word DOC file can be uploaded for the conversion to AZW.

The Last Perfect Father's Day is an example of an early Kindle book. In fact, go to Amazon search for several years, say 2007, 2009, 2011. Preview books published in the various years and see the improvement, especially in nonfiction. A lot has changed in the past decade. Now even the most whiz-bang interactive components of an e-book can be implemented with a little programming knowledge.

All of that said, with a willingness to learn rudimentary HTML code, an e-book can be dressed to the highest quality. It's not hard and needed resources can be found on the internet.

Who is doing the work?

I'm not going to assume that everyone who has bought this book will want to prepare and release a book themselves. After reading the details, some readers may choose to hire someone else.

Some aggregators, such as Smashwords, offer conversion work as part of the service. These are usually standardized methods and have some specific file requirements. Outside contractors can be hired to do the necessary formatting as well.

For those who are uncomfortable working with graphics, hiring someone to create the cover and internal graphics may be the best option. Graphics within some e-book formats require special handling as explained in Chapter 11.

Distribution channels

At one time, e-books were limited to PDF files distributed through a website or email. When the Kindle was introduced, compatible e-books had to be purchased at Amazon. With so many devices, we now have multiple distribution options. Each device has its own store: Amazon, Barnes & Noble, Kobo, and iBooks Store. Independent e-books stores, such as Smashwords. sell e-books in multiple formats and reach readers with all the various devices.

Plans for distribution, or the way the product is sold, may determine what file format(s) used. AZW files are needed for a good Kindle experience. But all devices can read a simple PDF. Questions such as where readers will be found and how they'll be reading the ebook need to be considered when determining product distribution.

The distribution decision should be considered early in the process. This will determine the file formatting later. Take time during the writing process to consider the various options.

If the plan is to exclusively sell the e-book on Amazon, iBooks, or other distributor, this decision should be made before finishing the work in progress. Each individual distributor has specific formatting "rules."

If the e-book is offered on a website with an affiliate program, the choices may be simpler.

Research and consider all the possibilities while writing. That way when the time comes to format and prepare the book, the correct process can be used. The e-book won't have to be re-formatted completely for each iteration.

Directly from Amazon, Apple App Store, etc.

Many authors have successfully worked directly with the various e-book retailers. If the choice is to distribute directly through the popular e-book sites, the first step is to read all the terms and conditions completely. Some of these are written in legalese and hard to understand, so get advice. (Since I'm not a lawyer, I won't be offering any.)

It's less costly if using only one online bookstore, say Amazon. There's nothing wrong with that strategy. It avoids the middleman cost with just a little effort. Many writers have successful careers with only Kindle books.

Amazon is rather straightforward to upload an e-product. Follow the instructions at **Kindle Direct Publishing** (KDP). Be sure it's polished and shining before uploading. As an editor, I tend to see minor problems in a publication. But the general public will see glaring issues like poor page formatting.

KDP now offers tools to create textbooks, kids' books, and graphic novels. For a nonfiction book heavy with images, one of these options may be best. Be aware, there's an additional cost each time a graphics-heavy e-book is downloaded.

For an Apple product, we have two choices: an iBook or an app. Most authors will choose an iBook. iBooks, Apple's e-book reader and store, is a bit more complicated than other distributors, but not impossible. Apple has more requirements than Amazon, but it is still certainly doable. For more information, read the **iBook FAQs**.

An app is primarily used for interactive books with audio and video content. iBooks Author, a free app from Apple, is designed to create iBooks with interactive features. It is, however, only available to those with the Mac Lion OS or higher. Also, an e-book created with iBooks Author can be sold only in the iBooks Store.

Understand that choosing to distribute exclusively through the iBook store means the e-book will be available only on Apple products. No iBook reader exists for Windows or Android devices.

Third Party Distributors (Aggregators)

Aggregators provide all types of services from formatting manuscripts to distribution through all the major e-book companies, and some stuff in between. Each one has a different fee structure. A couple even have packages that include printing hard copies along with e-distribution. Most aggregators don't have agreements with Amazon for distribution. A Kindle book will need to be handled separately.

These are worth looking at even when choosing the do-it-yourself path. A lot can be learned about the process, and free downloadable guides, which can help with formatting and marketing an e-product, are available.

Your Website

It's possible to sell an e-book, whether PDF, MOBI, or EPUB, from a website. The easiest way is with a PDF file. Microsoft Word, WordPerfect, and OpenOffice have an option to save a PDF file. Two things to consider: 1) Products may not have the same digital rights management (DRM) as those sold through

Amazon and Apple. 2) Customers will have to upload the product to their device manually.

Multiple versions of a book can be sold through the website either as a do-it-yourself or through a download service.

Many companies provide download services. The two popular ones are ClickBank and PayLoadz. Both companies have fees but also offer products that can added to a website store, which may complement your product.

Another option to sell on your website is to offer links to the book at Amazon, Barnes & Noble, or other online source.

E-products can be sold directly without using a download service. The do-it-yourself method, requires knowing some programming skills and the ability to monitor email often. A website shopping cart is also required. E-junkie and WooCommerec (a WordPress plug-in) are two popular carts. The advantage is more products than e-books, such as online classes, can be sold from a website with one tool.

In Person

A question often asked when talking about e-books is about selling them at the back of the room or in an exhibit area. Selling e-products in person is not as hard as it may seem.

One way is having the e-book available on a CD-ROM. Many personal computers have the ability to burn a CD. CD images and cover images are just as important for a CD as they are for a print book. **Kunaki.com** is a no nonsense service for printing the disc and covers for a CD or DVD. It does require some hands-on work by the user. The prices are more than reasonable.

A downloadable version can be sold in a variety of other ways. When using a shopping cart such as E-junkie, a code for the download can be created. The code can be printed on a bookmark or postcard to give to a buyer.

It's easier than I thought to order custom plastic cards, much like the gifts cards sold in stores. The cards can have a code and instructions under a scratch off area on the back. E-books can be sold in bookstores with these cards. For more information, read Dean Wesley Smith's blog article "**Electronic Sales to Bookstores**."

QR (Quick Response) codes can be printed on business cards or post cards to sell e-products. Some even make a poster so the QR code is large enough to read from a distance and the sale is handled through a smart phone. I use QR codes on my printed promotional material for links to my books and my newsletter. Some websites, such as Vista Print, have QR code generators to use to add to a product. Use Google to search for "QR code generators," to find resources for these codes.

Sidebars, pull quotes, and other extras

Sidebars, pull quotes, and footnotes present unique problems in an e-book. All are possible but require special handling during the formatting process. Since the reader is in control of a variety of options, which changes the appearance of an e- book, these special format options often don't work well. It's not the same as a static printed page, where the reader has no choice. When writing solely for e-publishing, don't include sidebars, pull quotes, and footnotes. There are other ways to handle this information, which will be discussed in Chapter 6. For those converting a manuscript formatted for print production, we'll also cover how to make changes in the file to accommodate these features.

While it may not be possible to have some standard print options in an e-book, extra information can be presented in other ways. Newer e-reader devices allow the author to add audio and video to the book. Whether it's a voice reading the text, a slide presentation, or a video, these extras are readily available. Additional information added in this way can greatly enhance the reader's experience.

Exclusivity

Apple and Amazon have two products that can make them the exclusive distributor. As I read the distribution statements with these products, it means we cannot sell our books on our own websites. There may be other distribution systems with exclusivity clauses in their contracts. We're looking at Apple and Amazon because they are more popular e-book sellers.

We've already looked at Apple's iBooks Author and the conditions for using it. Let's turn to Amazon.

Amazon offers **KDP Select**. This option makes an e-book available for the Kindle Lending Library offered to Amazon Prime Members, and it allows us to offer our book free for five days during the ninety-day contract period. KDP Select books may not be offered in any other format anywhere, including our own websites, during the contract period.

It is important to think about the matter of having an e-book in only one market. Don't wait and make a rash decision. Each author and each product is different and marketing may be different. The decision is more than reaching the widest market. It affects the entire marketing plan.

Karin Bilich discusses advantages, and a few negatives, of KDP Select in this article at Smart Authors Sites

Sharing

(Disclaimer: I'm not a lawyer. While I try to check legal matters with attorneys and legal websites, I'm not offering legal advice. If you have further legal questions, contact a literary attorney.)

When I was a novice writer I was unduly concerned about my work being "stolen." It was silly for me to think anyone would want to take credit for my early writing. This concern comes up more often with e-publications. To most people it seems easier to share, print, or otherwise acquire the product without a purchase.

Each one of us must decide if we want to allow people to lend our e-books to their friends? What about giving it to a friend? Think about it for a minute, sharing an e-book is different than a print book. A print book can't be used by the owner while loaning it or giving it to a friend. But an e-book can be on two devices at one time.

Amazon now has a program to lend Kindle books. All e-books are automatically enrolled in the lending program. Only those priced in the 35 percent royalty bracket can opt-out of the program. Amazon places limitations on reader-to-reader lending. For more information see "**Lending for Kindle**" at the KDP website.

Security and digital rights management can be added to any e-book including PDF files and Word DOCs, which limits reproduction of that book. Most of these schemes limit lending (except Kindle) and sharing. Some even limit ability to print the e-book.

Before we go further, I think it would be good to have a discussion of copyright violations, piracy and plagiarism. Here's what I've learned.

Copyright violation, piracy, or plagiarism is when our product is sold or given away without our permission. Plagiarism is "The act of appropriating the literary composition of another author, or excerpts, ideas, or passages therefrom, and passing the material off as one's own creation."[1] The Copyright Office says, "As a general matter, copyright infringement occurs when a copyrighted work is reproduced, distributed, performed, publicly displayed, or made into a derivative work without the permission of the copyright owner."[2]

So for clarity sake, when I talk about sharing, I'm not talking about any of these illegal activities. I'm talking about giving away or loaning my book with proper attribution. In the following comments, I believe that is what others are talking about as well.

Mark Coker, founder of Smashwords, says this, "DRM is counterproductive. If you don't trust your readers to honor your copyright, you'll reach fewer paid readers."

Thomas Umstattd, CEO of Castle Media Group, started quite a discussion on his blog, Author Media, with this post **"Authors: Piracy is Not Your Enemy."**

Before we end this section, I want to mention the Creative Common License. If you don't know about Creative Commons, **Umstattd has a clear explanation on his blog**.

I present this information to get you to thinking about how you would like to protect your book, if at all.

Which comes first: print or e-book?

Of course, every book producer will have an opinion. Many first-time book authors think the e-book should be first because it's inexpensive and faster to get to market. Some writers also plan to have only an e-book. Today it's the rare writer who will have only a print book.

My preference is to do my e-book first. I found it too time-consuming to remove all the print formatting for the e-book. Others go the other route. TR Fischer, author of *Prey for Me* and *A Man Around the House*, says, "Formatting the print book took me longer than the e-book. I would have formatted the print version first. The process of ordering a proof of the print book took longer than I anticipated with shipping time."

Not only is the order in which to publish a decision that shouldn't be left to the last minute, but also whether to publish both print and electronic should be thought about early. Each format has different considerations. Think: will this work as an e-book? How does the text formatting need to be changed to make my print book an e-book? Do elements of my e-book need to be changed for print? And should there even be a print edition?

Electronic books are stretching limits of technology. Amazon now has enhanced e-books with videos and audio. An enhanced version of *Harry Potter and the Sorcerer's Stone* has an owl flying on the cover. Google has introduced **Editions at Play**; books "powered by the magic of the internet." These books use Google maps and other internet apps to enhance the story. Will these developments make current e-readers obsolete? How many of you have unreadable 5-¼-inch floppy disks because the equipment is no longer standard or available? This may be a good reason to have a print book as well as e-book.

Move Forward

Decisions to start to think about now:

- ☐ Are you going to offer a print edition and an e-book at the same time?
- ☐ Are you going to include audio or video enhancements?
- ☐ Are you going to offer your e-book exclusively in one distribution channel?
- ☐ Check the various ways to sell and distribute your e-book and decide which you'll use.
- ☐ How are you going to distribute?
- ☐ Will you allow sharing?

End Notes

1. _____, "plagerism," The Free Dictionary, https://legal-dictionary.thefreedictionary.com/plagerism, accessed January 2, 2018.

2. _____, "Definitions," Copyright.gov, https://www.copyright.gov/help/faq/faq-definitions.html, accessed January 2, 2018.

CHAPTER FOUR

AMAZON PUBLISHING SERVICES

I n recent months Kindle Direct Publishing (KDP) has introduced more service to help indie-publishers create a Kindle book. Let's start with the newer services.

KDP Pricing Support

For years determining the price of an e-book has been part careful calculations, part art form, and a little magic. **KDP Pricing Support** was introduced last year and is still in beta (an early version of a product still being tested). It's a to tool, which uses various factors to compare a Kindle book with others in the Amazon system to suggest an ideal price. Some of the factors are category, number pages, and author's past sales. The service provides a chart that shows both author earnings and number of books sold at specific prices along with a recommended price. KDP help files includes "As price is just one of many factors that may affect sales of any title, please use your judgment when considering this data and setting the list price for your book."[1]

KDP Print

CreateSpace is Amazon's print-on-demand service. Last year, Amazon introduced a beta version of **creating a print version directly through KDP**. Some observers believe this is prelude to the two services merging. After publishing a Kindle book, users are given the opportunity to start the publishing a print book. This is service is also still in beta. As this option has been used more services are being added such as author copy discount. Although explained differently, the royalties are about the same. At the time of this writing, KDP Print is still getting mixed reviews from users.

Kindle Jumpstart

Amazon describes **Jumpstart** as a "simple, step-by-step guide to publishing on Amazon." Included in the guide are 12 step-by-step topics, videos, activities, "insider tips," and webinars. Insider tips lead the user to other KDP help articles. Jumpstart naturally leads the user to Amazon services such as the cover creator (resources). Although lacking details of such things as formatting, it's a good overview of the process.

Kindle Create (KC)

The recently (Fall 2017) released **Kindle Create** is described as a way to "transform your completed manuscript into a beautiful kindle eBook."[2] It can be used as a stand-alone program or an add-in (Windows only). The Mac version is a stand-alone software only. The program uses DOC/DOCX files for flowing Kindle books and PDF files for fixed format books. KC is not a complete formatting program. It uses four different templates to add little details such as title styles. Although described as "simple," manuscripts still require a lot of the formatting details found in this book. (Read my assessment at Practical Inspirations **http://practicalinspirations.com/kindle-create-not-ready-for-prime-time/**)

Amazon has offered a number of other services for e-book publishers. Some, such as Cover Creator, have been mentioned in other parts of this book. Here's some more to consider.

Comic Creator

Comic Creator is a downloaded software used to convert illustrated books, such as graphic novels, to Kindle KF8 files to upload to KDP. The software comes in two version: one with a previewer, one without. Like other Amazon publishing tools, the program has limitations.

Kindle Kids' Book Creator

This downloaded app is similar to Comic Creator in that it handles illustrated books. Artwork can be uploaded in popular formats: PDF, JPG, GIF, PNG, and TIFF. Full book PDF files can also be used. It allows text to be added to the pages as well as text pop-ups.

Kindle Textbook Creator

Again, **a downloaded tool** to covert PDF files to a fixed layout Kindle book. Media files, audio, video, and images, can be added as icon links or hot links connected to text. Textbook Creator is very similar to Kindle Create. Books published with Textbook Creator can be designated as a textbook by using "kdp_textbook_submission" as a keyword.

(Please note: Kindle Create, Comic Creator, Kindle Kids' Book Creator, and Kindle Textbook Creator are subject to Amazon's Software End Users License Agreement. Books created with these products can only be sold through the Kindle store.)

X-Ray for Authors

X-Ray allows readers to access additional information in short comments by pressing on a term in the book. The information may be author comments or Wikipedia articles. X-Ray may be added after publication. **Here's details of adding X-Ray.**

Kindle Book Lending

Kindle book owners may lend their books to family and friends for a period of fourteen days. The book is unreadable on the owner's device. All Kindle books are enrolled in the lending library by default. Books in the 35% royalty option have a choice to opt-out of the lending library.

Kindle Matchbook

Matchbook is an opportunity to offer a Kindle book at a reduced price ($2.99 or less) when the print edition has been purchased. Enrollment in this program is through KDP.

KDP Select

This **optional program** offers promotional tools not available outside the program. These tools are Kindle Countdown Deal and Free Book Promotion. Books enrolled in Select are also available in the Kindle Unlimited program, which is a pay service for customers. Enrollment in Unlimited allows the user to read a book free of charge. Royalties are paid from a global fund based on number of pages read. Kindle books enrolled are exclusive to Amazon.

Audio Creation Exchange (ACX)

Amazon sells digital audio books through **Audible Audiobooks**. **ACX** is the service for creating an audio book. Authors can narrate their own book or hire a professional narrator. The cost of narration is negotiated between the author and narrator. ACX makes audio books available through Audible, Amazon, and iTunes. Audios created through ACX are also available for Whispersync recordings within a Kindle book. Royalties are up to 40 percent.

There are a number of little known Amazon services that author/publishers can use to promote their books.

Amazon Advantage

With this service, Amazon will stock print books for immediate shipping. The author or publisher is required to provide products to Amazon. The book will be listed as "in stock," which is often shown higher in the search results.

Author Central

Author Pages are handled through **Author Central**. Author Pages allow us to have our biography, list of upcoming events, and RSS feed to our blogs. All books, including anthologies, are listed on the page as well. Readers can also follow an author through the Author Page.

Amazon Associates

This is **Amazon's affiliate program**. Affiliate programs allow website owners to earn a small commission on products sold through affiliate links on that website. We can use Associate links for our own books, as well as books we review or mention, to earn a small commission on those products.

End Notes

1. _____, "KDP Pricing Support (Beta)," Kindle Direct Publishing, https://kdp.amazon.com/en_US/help/topic/ G201551180, accessed 12-27-2017.

2. _____, "Kindle Create," Kindle Direct Publishing, https://kdp.amazon.com/en_US/help/topic/ GHU4YEWXQGNLU94T. accessed 12-27-2018

CHAPTER FIVE

WHILE YOU WRITE

I wrote my first book for the limited market attending my speaking gigs. The second, however, was intended for wider distribution. Up until this time, my primary writing was for magazines, anthologies, or other publications where I didn't worry about some of the tiny details it takes to publish a book. While some of these details may not be needed for all e-book publications, it's a good idea to at least learn about them. Honestly, I hadn't done my homework the first time around.

While writing our books, we can work on some of the details. Each one of these can be accomplished while the book is in progress or while the editor is working on it. After pounding on the keyboard all the day, take some time to take care of these niggly details.

Why? Every writer is anxious to get the finished product out to the world. Trying to take care of these details after writing and formatting may cause the tendency to rush the process and have to correct mistakes later.

All books will need certain information no matter whether it is published for a small market or a large distribution company. Some of these items will seem like no-brainers, but some thought is needed before hitting the publish button.

Title

Go ahead; roll your eyes. I'm sure most of us understand our books need a title. A title is more than just the name of the book. It's also a description, a marketing tool, and adds to the personality of the book. Let's look at some of the keys to a good book title.

When a book is published through a traditional publisher, the editorial committee often selects the title. For most indie-published e-book writers, the decision is ours. Choose the title carefully. While writing, jot down title ideas as they come and cull through them later. Social media followers enjoy being part of the publishing process; ask for their suggestions. The title is important, so don't rush the process

Short: Three or four words are about all that's needed. A complete summary of the book isn't need in the title. One reason for a short title, especially for an e-book, is to be able to make those words large enough to be read on a nearly postage stamp graphic online. The cover will be competing with hundreds of others on the screen. Long titles aren't easily read, and the reader's eye will pass right over the book.

If the title needs added information, add a subtitle. Or ask the designer to emphasize the main words of a long title. One example is a Kindle book titled ***How to Publish and Sell Your Article on Kindle***. The largest words on the cover are "Your Article on Kindle." Those words capture the attention of potential readers, who may click on the cover and see the entire title.

- Clear: Don't be cute or coy with the title. The reader doesn't want to try to decipher the meaning of it. If the title isn't clear, the reader won't trust you. Trust between author and reader is essential to word-of-mouth advertising. Even if when writing fiction, the title needs to clearly represent the story. If the book *Your Article on the Kindle* were titled something like *The Karma of Article Publishing*, book browsers probably wouldn't understand what the book is about. And those who don't believe in karma may not even want to read the book at all.

- Keywords: The title can help readers find a book through a search engine. Think about the words readers may use to search and see if those fit in your title. Guess which of the titles above will be at the top of list when "writing article Kindle" are the terms used for a search? Do be cautious not to overthink this and try to use keywords just for search engine ranking. More on keywords in Appendix 6.

Description

Write two book descriptions. This should actually be completed before the first sentence is typed. As a part of preparing to write the book, write a description of the idea–a thesis statement, if you will. This will be the place to return to when writer's block hits.

- Short description: The short description can also become the elevator pitch used when asked what the book is about. This description will also be used for the product description. It should be concise and include keywords.

- Long description: The long description is the back cover copy on a print book. It can also be used on a website and other sites such as Goodreads to describe the book. The long description is also good for press releases and when asking for reviews.

Categories

Every distribution channel asks what category/genre the book should be placed in. Think of this as the Dewey Decimal number for the online bookstore. Give it careful thought. Look at similar books and see what categories they're in.

These categories also help with keyword searches. However, for the searches to be effective, we need to know our target audience. If writing a book about gardening with children, the target audience is parents and grandparents. A secondary audience may be teachers or gardeners.

Categories can also be used on a blog. I have a category for e-books. When I write a post about e-books, I use that category to send all of my e-book posts to one page.

Keywords

We often think of keywords as applying to web content. Because an e-book is primarily sold on the internet, keywords are used not only by the bookstore, but also helps readers find it in an online search. Keywords are the terms readers are most likely to use when looking for a specific topic. Kindle Direct Publishing (KDP) allows up to seven keywords. (Hint: A keyword can be more than one word, as in "e-book formatting.")

Fiction has keywords also. Fiction keywords will include the genre plus setting (Georgia and Revolutionary War, for example), popular tie-ins (zombies, apocalypse), or other details. Again, check books in the same genre to see what keywords are being used.

Cover

I recommend beginning to research cover possibilities now. Even if a graphic artist is creating the cover, that person will need some specific directions. For one of my books, although I hired a graphic artist to create the cover. I found the photo I wanted and specified the typeface to be used. In other words, I knew the look I wanted but needed a designer to put it all together for me.

Take a look through various e-book stores. The standout covers are those similar to a print book cover. The eye quickly skips the standard e-book cover. For a look at some award winning covers, check **The Book Designers** award list for cover ideas. Most have comments about what works and what doesn't.

Amazon has a free cover creator. However, I find the cover options bland and the e-book wouldn't stand out against a professionally designed cover. I do suggest going through the exercise of using the creator to get an idea of what the difference between a stock cover and a designed cover can be.

Test the cover with potential readers. Have a give-away for those who vote or maybe a double give-away that includes something for those who offer suggestions. (The same can be done with the book title.)

Typically, the back cover of a print book is as important as the front cover. Not true with an e-book because there is no back cover. The back cover generally has a book description and a couple of endorsements. The same information used for a print book can be used elsewhere in an e-book. The description can be used for the online catalog. Endorsements can be added to the end of the book. Better yet, ask endorsers to write a review on Amazon or other platforms where it's more visible and can have more influence on potential readers.

Once an idea for the cover is born, hire a graphic artist design it. Don't wait until it's time to upload the book. Don't even wait until formatting is started. It may take several weeks to finalize the cover. Allow some back and forth time with the graphic artist, plus the time needed for the work to be done.

The sooner the cover is ready, the sooner it can be used for marketing. The cover image can be used for pre-publication marketing.

Marketing

I'm sure we've heard this more times than we've heard that we should hire a professional editor: begin to build our platform and market before our book is published. Entire books have been written about marketing books. Every one I've read tells the writer to start marketing before the book is finished. Some experts may even say to begin before starting to write the book.

It's true. And it's hard. I know I often get into my writing zone, sometimes for several days and don't want to take the time to even send a Tweet about my progress. Forget writing a blog post. Already today, I had a great idea for a Facebook comment. I didn't do it or write it down while I was thinking about it. I went on with my writing. Yep, you guessed it, the good idea is gone. (I'll look around on the floor to see if that idea fell out of my brain.)

One way to start marketing early is to write blog posts or magazine articles about the topic of the book. It's possible to judge reader interest in a topic. These articles can also be the starting point of chapters.

Social media is considered by many as one of the fastest ways to spread the word about a book. In addition to Facebook and Twitter, now there's Pinterest, Goodreads, and Periscope. These are important but time-consuming marketing resourses. Social media marketing needs to be planned, scheduled, and done.

No social media accounts? Get at least one now. I recommend starting with Facebook. It's easier to get started with and to keep up with, although other writers prefer Twitter as a starting point.

For those who are active on social media, at least start dropping hints about writing a book. Talk about the progress, the topic, and even ask for encouragement and accountability.

We'll have more marketing ideas in Chapter 6.

Set up accounts

We need various accounts to publish our e-books. Once we've determine the way to distribute our e-books, set up the appropriate accounts now. Those who are planning to use **Smashwords**, take a moment now to set up the account and learn the system. Those who are planning to do their own distribution should get those accounts now — Kindle, Nook, Apple (**iBookStore requires an application and approval**). (See Appendix 3 for instructions to set up a KDP account.)

When we wait until it's time to hit the publish button, we sometimes get in a hurry, then frustration can set in, mistakes made, and the process is slowed down.

Other Types of Accounts

- **Library of Congress (LOC).** The Library of Congress creates a catalog database used by librarians to locate specific items. We may miss a key market opportunity without a listing in this database. LOC will assign a number prior to publication, which can be added to the copyright page.

- **Copyright.** The United States Copyright Office registers the copyright of publications, videos, audios, and other creative works. It is true that you own the copyright of written products as soon as the words are in tangible form, whether it be an email, a blog post, or a computer file. Copyright registration is highly recommended in case of legal challenges.

  Two copies of the "best edition" of the publication must be sent to the Copyright Office. E-book are sent with the copyright application. Two copies of a print book are mailed after submitting the application.

  Even though copyright registration isn't done until after the book is completed, having as much information as possible beforehand eases the process.

- **ISBN.** ISBN uniquely identifies a book to facilitate bookstore sales. When ISBN number(s) are purchased, the publication is automatically included in **Bowker's Books in Print** listing. Each format of a book will require an individual ISBN. Numbers can be purchased singly, in groups of ten, or groups of 100. Unless you have no other books to write (Really? You're going to write only one book?), the group of ten is the most cost-effective. The ISBN needs to be purchased before publication so it can be included on the copyright page, with a barcode on the cover of a print book, and with a KDP account.

For those publishing from a country, other than the United States, an ISBN is obtained from an agency in that country. Locate the appropriate agency at the **International ISBN Agency** website.

Price

Begin researching price options. What are other e-books in the same field priced at? Don't go too far over, and don't try to undercut. (Think back to the step of having a good book. The work put into writing a good book is worth a fair price.) Indie publishers have the option of raising or lowering prices at anytime. Chapter 6 has details for determining price.

Website/blog

This is one of our primary marketing tools. Get it going early. It's not necessary to know all the background coding to have a good-looking website. Using a content management system (CMS) or blog platform, such as WordPress, makes it easy for anyone. There is a learning curve; we don't want to be learning to do this at the moment our product is going out to the world. Writing for our blogs or websites can relieve writer's block as well. For some of us, building a website may be more than we want to tackle. If that's the case, hire someone to do the internet work.

Move Forward

Do one of these each day as a break from writing.

- ☐ Ask for advice or suggestions for your title.
- ☐ Look for possible cover graphics.
- ☐ Make a list of the categories your book fits in.
- ☐ Research and brainstorm keywords.
- ☐ Set up your accounts for LOC, ISBN, and distribution companies (Kindle, Barnes & Noble, iBooks, etc.).
- ☐ Research the price of books in the same niche.
- ☐ If you don't have a website, start setting it up.
- ☐ Write a marketing plan.

Now back to writing.

CHAPTER SIX

OTHER PRE-PUBLICATION CONSIDERATIONS

Pricing

Here's a list of some of the most expensive Kindle books I found.

- *Encyclopedia of Language and Linguistics (Second Edition 2005)* $11,850 (http://amzn.to/2hLco3J)

- *International Encyclopedia of Social & Behavioral Sciences (First Edition 2001)* $16,870 (http://amzn.to/2iKGfeo)

- The winner is multi-volume *Collier Encyclopedia on Bankruptcy* (Release 149, December 2016) $11,519 *each*. Yes, that price is for each one of the reported 29 volumes. (http://amzn.to/2iWBmhM)

I haven't decided if pricing of an e-book is a fine science, a matter of luck, or both. Both of my PDF books are priced at $4.95.

One has done moderately well, but the other hasn't. I know that I need to do some readjusting and different marketing.

Looking through my consumer glasses, I don't want to pay close to the same price for an e-book as I do for a print edition. Most of us don't want to pay nearly the same price for a pile of electrons as we do for a tangible product. One of my editing clients has the e-book version of their leading title priced only $5.00 less than the print edition. The organization has been disappointed in e-book sales.

Many traditional publishers are using e-books as a way to shore up falling print profits. In that quest, some e-books cost more than the print edition. I'm not sure how effective that strategy is for the self-publisher or small press. A May 2016 report at Author Earnings says the Big Five are steadily lowering e-book prices.[1]

An interesting note, two of the above books are available in hard cover for less than $200 each. It would be interesting to see the sales information on those titles.

Looking through my self-publisher glasses, I know the primary cost of my e-book is very low compared to the print edition. Actually, there's almost no cost for materials once the hard work of writing is completed. This fact probably clouds my consumer glasses.

Search the internet for "pricing e-books" and a number of lists with several different theories will be listed. Some factors do seem to rise to the top. (There is a few articles in Appendix 7.)

The Audience

Knowing the audience for a book is important when writing and when pricing. A writer or publisher needs to know what the target audience will pay for specific topics and genres. Business books, whether print or electronic, tend to cost more than general how-to books or novels. One of my target audiences is homeschool families. I know they primarily have one income, so don't have a lot of extra money to spend on non-essential items. (And yes, I have to admit my books are non-essential.)

The Competition

Check the price of books with a similar theme. This gives an indication of what the audience is willing to pay. Pricing slightly lower than the average or the same price may be the best strategy.

The new KDP Pricing Support gives the average price of similar books.

The Cost

Selling e-books costs money. Books sold through Amazon or iBookstore require a payment of a fee for each book sold. Amazon has set their "royalty" to encourage certain pricing. Most fees are a percentage of the retail price. When using an aggregator, there may be an upfront cost, which needs to be recouped before making a profit.

One advantage with e-books is that if the price isn't working, it can be easily changed. Some say it's a bad idea to lower the price because those who buy at the higher price will be upset. If the price fluctuates too often that can be a result. I consider that everything whether a car or an e-book has discounted prices at some point.

Free is, of course, an option as well. There are a number of good reasons to price an e-book at zero. Many authors offer the first of a series as a free download to promote their other products. Temporary free offers are used to promote a new book. Many self-publishers report sales go up after a free promo. Smashwords also reports that free e-books get 100 times more downloads. This greatly improves word-of-mouth advertising. Amazon has Kindle Match program, which allows the Kindle version to be offered at a reduced price—including free—with the purchase of the print edition. Offering the Kindle version free is an opportunity for book promotion.

As we see, pricing an e-book can be "rocket science" and there's no magic formula. The best research is reviewing what similar products are selling for, and adjusting from there.

When I write a book on bankruptcy law, I can look at the most expensive Kindle book and get an idea of a good price for it.

Two good articles on e-book pricing:

- **10 Things to Consider When Pricing E-books**

- **How much should an ebook cost?**

Marketing

If you have read this far and not thought about marketing, stop now and go begin marketing. Marketing can't wait until the book is completed. Just telling family and friends isn't enough. The rest of the world needs to know as well.

I made that mistake in the past. I was afraid if I started advertising (and marketing really is advertising, but we shy away from the word), and didn't meet my self-imposed deadline or somehow the book didn't get finished (floods happen), then I would have failed. I thought if a catastrophe happened, no one would ever want to read anything I wrote again.

Marketing an e-book is much the same as marketing a traditionally-published book. Even if the book is published through a traditional publisher, marketing is the writer's job. This is not a book about marketing. There are dozens of very good ones, and I've listed those in the resources at the end of this book. There are marketing techniques to use while writing and formatting.

Through Your Website

As discussed in Chapter 3 on distribution, there are a number of ways to sell an e-product on a website. It can be as simple as using links to Amazon, Smashwords, or other distributor. Or MOBI, EPUB, and other formats can be created to download.

Considering what formats to offer is a decision that needs to be made prior to publishing time.

Putting an e-book on a website won't generate sales; we must build the buzz needed for buyers to know the product is available. A blog has become one of the most common ways now. Another marketing method I've found useful is offering a free chapter. I offer free chapters of my e-books as a PDF file, which can be downloaded directly from my website.

If we've heard it once, we've heard eight or nine times: A newsletter is a must for marketing. The newsletter needs to be regular and not always have the same content as a blog or the book. My newsletter always has something only for newsletter subscribers. A newsletter is often the first place to announce a book release.

There are several ways to set up a e-newsletter. Yahoo Groups or Google Groups can be used. These are primarily known for group email discussions. But, they do have an "announcement only" feature, which can be used for a newsletter. They've placed limitations on how subscriptions are gathered and on adding subscribers. If the newsletter list is large, some email outlets won't allow multiple recipients in the TO or BCC box. Yahoo and Google are strictly manual, no automation.

Plus, all the formatting must be done by hand or the content must be limited to text only. That is not always a bad option. Chris Brogan, best-selling author, professional speaker, and owner of Owner Media Group, says, "I'm a much bigger fan of plain text and/or very simple HTML formats over very pretty formatting. People aren't getting your information based on the fact it looks like a gorgeous web page in their inbox. They want to read it."[2]

Email newsletter services abound. **Mail Chimp** offers free service for those with a small email list. **A simple list of free email services** is found in Appendix 8. Some web hosting companies have newsletter functions as well. Check with the hosting company to see what is offered.

Social Media

There are so many social media channels available it's easy to spend all day, every day trying to keep up, and still fall behind. Dozens of books are available about ways to use social media to drive traffic to a website or sell books. Plus, we could spend an entire week talking about them.

The two most popular today are Facebook and Twitter, with Pinterest coming up quickly. I recommend being on at least Facebook and Twitter. The two accounts can be linked so posting to one posts to the other at the same time.

Services, such as **HootSuite** and **Buffer**, to automate social media posts. I do have a peeve about using the auto-posting services. There is no direct contact with the reader. It's too easy to just push out thoughts (or a sales pitch) without spending time interacting with friends and followers. Always remember the "social" part.

Pinterest is becoming more talked about as a marketing tool

for authors. I've not used my Pinterest account for marketing, although I do have boards on the topics I write and speak about. Not only is time a factor, also I haven't quite figured out how to best use Pinterest for marketing my books. I have a Pin It button on my website and do get notices when my posts are being pinned. Before using it as a marketing tool, consider **an article from an attorney** about copyright issues. For more discussions about copyright and Pinterest, do an internet search for "lawyer why not use pinterest."

On the other side, Laura Christianson at Blogging Bistro has a **series about Pinterest.** (At the time of this writing, the link for the recommended e-book wasn't working.) Ms. Christianson has several how-to posts for Pinterest.

Writer's Digest published an article "How to Use Pinterest to Market Your Book".

Other social media channels include Google+, LinkedIn, Goodreads, and Periscope. Details about using each of these outlets on the internet.

Using the Crowd

No, I don't mean "cloud;" I mean "crowd." This means involving relatives, neighbors, and friends. Because the business of writing is viewed as glamorous, people like to feel a part of the adventure. Often, all it takes is asking them to help.

Beta readers are non-professionals who read books and give

feedback about the manuscript before publication. They provide comments about readabilty, clarity, usefulness, and marketablity.

I met an editor at a conference who has a group of beta readers she can call on to read manuscripts for her clients. Where does she find these people? She asks. If she sees someone reading a specific genre at a bookstore or coffee shop, she asks if they would like to preview books. In online groups and at social events, she keeps her ears open for readers and what they like to read. Beta readers often become the first to review and recommend a book.

Goodreads has groups for writers to **find beta readers**. A local critique group can be a source for beta readers. For more information about beta readers Chuck Sambuchino has two *Writer's Digest* articles:

- **What Are Beta Readers? And Do You Need Them?**

- **Peer Reviews: Seek Quality in Your Beta Readers, Not Quantity**

Belinda Pollard offers **"How to find a beta reader"** on her blog. Another way to involve the crowd is to get advice from social media. I asked members of several Facebook groups about title possibilities for this book. These people are now engaged. This can be a first step to marketing a book that's not finished. I have a place to start keeping people updated. The same method can be and has been used by writers for book covers, character names, and even deciding whether a character should live or not.

Blogging an upcoming book is another way to engage readers

before release. I've posted bits and pieces of information from this book on my blog. I don't say, "Here's another section of my book." I just post the information and see the reaction. Some writers do blog the entire book. Nina Amir discusses blogging a book at **howtoblogabook.com**.

Some fiction writers set up Facebook and Twitter accounts for characters in their stories. The reader can have an ongoing conversation with those characters. This technique can be used to drop hints of upcoming sequels. Lauraine Snelling has a website for the setting of her Blessings series, **www.blessingnd.com**.

Crowdsourcing, also called crowdfunding, is becoming very popular for financing all sorts of projects, including books. The idea is to ask people to contribute various amounts of money in exchange for perks. The perks are based on the level of monetary gift.

This also a way to include the crowd in the production and launch of a book. In other words, crowdsourcing can be a marketing tool. To be successful, crowdsourcing requires a well-planned campaign.

Mary DeMuth successfully funded her one of her books, *Not Marked*, with crowdsourcing. Review her **crowdsourcing webpage**, to get an idea of what is involved. Be sure to take a look at the update section. In the early part of the campaign, Ms. DeMuth had daily updates.

Prerelease campaign

Smashwords recently announced the asset-less preorder. An author can begin prerelease sales without the book actually being written. According to **the announcement article**, books with a preorder campaign earn three times as much as those without prerelease offer. If this is correct, a prerelease campaign might be worth the effort.

KDP also has a preorder option. The requirements include uploading a draft of the manuscript and other specifics.

Prerelease offers are usually priced lower than the price will be on day of release. Pre-sales, or preorders, is not a new technique or limited to e-books. Books by celebrity authors are often available for preorder.

All the marketing techniques listed require time and effort. Each possibility needs to be considered prior to hitting the publish button. It's a good idea to get started as soon as possible.

Diana Horner offers questions she asks her clients in **"How to Choose Self-Publishing Distribution Options for E-books."**

Move Forward

☐ Research the prices of books in your niche and determine the price of your e-book.

☐ Make a list of ways to begin marketing your book now.

☐ Set up an e-newsletter and start seeking subscribers.

☐ Begin to tell your friends on social media about your book. If you don't have a Facebook and Twitter account, set them up now.

☐ Look at crowdfunding website to determine if you want to use this for your book project.

☐ Research the various distribution options. Determine what you plan to use and set up accounts.

End Notes

1. "Data Guy," "A May 2016 look at Big Five ebook pricing," Author Earnings, June 2, 2016, http://authorearnings.com/big-five-may-2016-ebook-pricing/, accessed March 21, 2017.

2. Brogan, Chris, 2012, "Email Marketing Tips," June 15, 2012, http://chrisbrogan.com/inbox/

CHAPTER SEVEN

THE FOUNDATION

As we to get down to some of the details of preparing an e-book for publication, we need to understand some technicalities. Don't worry, it isn't necessary to be a programming or design expert. We only need a little knowledge of what an e-book really is.

Unlike print books, e-books aren't based on pages. They are actually one long flowing document. The reading device and user preferences determine the "pages" as the book is viewed. For this reason, page numbers and headers/footers aren't used in an e-book. There's no way for the e-reader to know where to place them.

E-books are also based on HTML programming code. This is the basic code used for web pages. Again, it isn't necessary to learn programming. We only need to understand that some of what we generally think of as standard formatting won't work. *Lulu Complete E-book Creator Guide*[1] states, "If it's not on your keyboard then it may not convert properly."[1] However, if we have some basic knowledge of HTML programming it may be possible to tweak the document a little more.

We're going to look at some of the basic elements in an e-book. Some of these are the same as a print book; others aren't.

Elements of an e-book

In addition to the details discussed in the previous chapter, two other elements aren't thought of as important e-book elements: font and file name.

Font

(I understand typeface is the technical term for what I'm discussing. However, with common usage in the electronic world the terms have become interchangeable. I will use the term font, which means a computer program that represents a typeface, for all references here.)

Generally, for ease of reading, whether in print or electronically, serif fonts are used for the body and sans serif is used for headlines and sub-heads. Serif fonts have the small decorative lines on the letters. Times Roman is a serif font. Sans serif fonts don't have the decorations. Arial is a common sans serif font, as shown here.

I would guess there are thousands of serif and sans serif fonts now available, not to mention the decorative fonts like Old English and Script. Save the decorative fonts for specific uses. Because e-books don't handle these fonts well, don't plan on the decorative fonts anywhere—even the cover. Stick to basics for an e-book. Times New Roman for the body text is generally accepted and converts well to all formats. Arial or Helvetica are a standard for headlines and sub-heads and also converts well.

Children's books follow the same idea. While a font that looks like a crayon mark or felt marking pen may be cute, it's harder for young eyes to read. Take a look at reading textbooks. They use the same serif and sans serif combination. One reason for this is the serifs on the body text allow the eye to naturally flow from one letter to the next, and from one word to the next.

Another consideration when selecting fonts is whether bold and italic will be used. Word allows all fonts to be set in bold or italic with the buttons on the menu bar. However, fonts have "family members." Another way to put it is "font style." If the selected font doesn't have bold, italic, or other style family members, the style may not translate when converted to a Kindle book. Most standard fonts have various style family members. Use the Font selection in the Format menu, not the font and style buttons found on the menu ribbon. Check the dropdown menu under "Font Style" to be sure the style needed is listed. If bold, italic, or underline are not in this list, those styles aren't part of the font family.

Remember, we want our readers to have a good experience, beginning with the ease of reading.

File Name

File name? How could that be important? Aren't people going to just see just the book title?

We never really know how our reader is going to download an e-book. If it's only offered on Amazon, iBooks, or other online stores, the file name may not be an issue. But if we're going to offer our e-books through other outlets, including websites, the file name can mean the difference between our book being read and ending up in the electronic trash bin. This is especially true of PDF files. If a PDF file is being read on a computer, the user may not see the cover, only the file name.

I own an e-book titled "BPTRBW" as the file name. After opening it a number of times to see what it is, I now remember what book it is. But the file name tells me nothing.

Quite simply, name the file the same as the title. I recommend not including any subtitles to make it easy for a reader to find on a computer or e-reader. It also isn't necessary to add the words "ebook" to a file name.

Use a "clean" file name. We often label our files by version or date. Many of us will label the final document with FINAL in the file name. While this is good for us to keep track of the many versions, it's unnecessary for our readers. Have a file simply named with the title of the book for public consumption.

One final caution: Don't leave spaces in the file name, such as "Create an e-Book." Some distribution centers or web servers can't read a file with spaces. It can be confusing to have one long word, "createane-book." Using upper case letters may help in an electronic file folder, "CreateAne-Book," but sometimes another system may convert it all to lower case letters, which can create an unusual word, such as "Ane." The best course of action is add hyphens or underscores, such as "Create_an_e-Book."

Covers

We've already talked about the importance of a good cover. The cover may be more important than the opening paragraph. If the reader isn't attracted to the book by the cover, they'll never read the first paragraph. How do we determine whether a cover is good for an e-book? Let's stop here for a little exercise.

Go to Amazon or another e-book seller. Search for a topic of interest. Search for a title on the same subject as your book. Now glance—only glance—t the screen. Which book does your eye gravitate to immediately? Now compare that cover to the others on the screen. What attracted you? The color? The graphic? The title? This little exercise should give a sense of the importance of the e-book cover. It's significant enough not to leave until publication time.

Try to avoid stock images, such as found in the Kindle Cover Creator. We don't want the cover to look like any other cover. Even those of us with some graphic arts skills should hire a graphic artist. We're writers; we should stick to that. For my book, ***Preschool: At What Cost?,*** I had a vision of the message I wanted my cover to send. I found a photo, purchased the license, then hired a graphic artist to manipulate it and add the text. It cost less than $100.

Content

I recently asked for a refund on a 99-cent Kindle book. Why? Because it had no useable content. It was merely an advertisement for an upcoming book. I won't buy the upcoming book either. I don't trust the writer. While I don't want to belabor the point of good, well-edited content, the truth is e-books won't be successful if it doesn't have good writing.

Don't shortchange the reader, or yourself, by rushing through or trying questionable marketing techniques. A well-written manuscript builds trust with readers and adds to our credibility for future projects.

Photos, Graphics, Sidebars, Pull Quotes

Generally, fiction doesn't have any of these elements. Except glyphs may be used at the beginning of a chapter or between scenes. But a novel usually won't have photos, graphics, sidebars, or pull quotes. A historical fiction I read recently included photos of the real people in the book—a rare exception. Photos and graphics require specific formatting for e-books.

Nonfiction books may not only have photos and graphics, but sidebars and pull quotes as well. One of the dangers with an e-book is thinking it's merely a print book on a screen. Remember, it's more like a long web page. The elements of a sidebar and pull quotes are handled completely differently. In general, sidebars or pull quotes won't be used. Not only is the formatting tricky, they can also interfere with the reading experience. We will discuss the how-to in a later chapter.

I find this to be another reason to prepare an e-book before the print book. Fewer of these elements need to be cleaned up.

Table of Contents and Index

The table of contents (TOC) can become more than a way to navigate through a document; it can actually become a marketing tool. The table of contents is often viewable in previews of the book. This is one of the first places I look when making a book-buying decision, whether online or in a brick and mortar store. Give careful thought to the TOC. Unlike holding a physical copy of the book, readers can't really skim an e-book. The TOC tells the reader what to expect.

If a print edition has already been formatted, the table of contents will be changed in the process of e-book formatting. It can either be removed to start over, or be changed when the time comes. If there are a lot of subheads, the best option may be to scrap it and start over.

Often an index isn't included in an e-book. Search features tend to take the place of an index. It's time consuming to create all of the links. An academic or reference book may need an index, but generally readers will use the search feature.

Front Matter

Other than the title page and copyright page, most of what we generally put in the front of a book should be moved or removed. Amazon and Barnes & Noble provide previews of e-books. They use the first few pages, generally 10 percent, including title and copyright pages. The sample should contain as much of the content as possible. If those few pages are filled with extraneous material, sales may be lost.

What do we do with those glowing reviews and endorsements, the acknowledgment page, and about the author? Put them in the back of the book. Think for a moment, how often do readers begin reading with these pages? I rarely even look at endorsements when considering purchasing a book. I may scan to see who has endorsed, but I don't read them. These comments should be in the review section of the online sales page and on a website. We'll discuss reviews and endorsements in the marketing chapter. One author has told me that placing a few comments at the beginning of the e-book is helpful, but she prefers the longer ones in the back.

Some e-book designers recommend putting the table of contents in the back of the book as well. I asked members of my Creating and Formatting e-Books class for editors, what they thought of putting the table of contents in the back. The consensus was for nonfiction, the table of contents is definitely needed in the preview. A couple people suggested a condensed TOC in the front, chapter titles only, with the complete TOC with subheads in the back. Most agree a TOC is unimportant for fiction.

On the other hand, Bridgette Powers, a fantasy writer, commented "[In] many YA [Young Adult] and speculative fiction novels (fantasy in particular), chapters do have titles, and I always like to browse those before purchasing. As a fantasy author who uses chapter titles to create another "hook" for the reader, I would include the TOC up front in hopes of further enticing readers."

Move Forward

☐ Save your manuscript file with the title of your book.

☐ Narrow cover image options to three. Ask followers on social media for comments.

☐ Prepare the front matter material.

End Notes

1. Woodward, David, 2011, *Lulu Complete eBook Creator Guide,* 2012, Lulu Press, http://connect.lulu.com/t5/eBook-Formatting-Publishing/eBook-Creator-Guide/ta-p/109443

CHAPTER EIGHT

BASIC STEPS TO FORMATTING

I'm sure you've been wondering when I'll get down to business. For those who skipped right to this chapter, I urge you to at least skim the previous chapters or look at the Move Forward sections.

Now, let's start some essential steps. But a word or two before we begin:

- Don't make these changes for a PDF formatted e-book (PDF instructions are in the appendix), and

- Be sure to make a backup of the completed file.

No matter the distribution plan for a book, certain formatting steps that need to be taken to prepare the manuscript. We will start with the content because it's the heart of our e-book.

Let's begin

While each of us may have a favorite word processor, Microsoft Word has become a standard used for many applications. For example, Smashwords uses a Word DOC as the basis for their conversion process. Now other products have added components to make converting to an e-book easier. Adobe's InDesign and Apple's Pages have an EPUB format export feature. The popular writing program Scrivener also has a way to compile the various parts into an EPUB format. Kindle now accepts unzipped EPUB files for conversion to Kindle-friendly files. It's not one of the preferred methods and may result in converting problems. Most self-publishers upload a Word DOC file.

With that in mind, the instructions will be given for a Word document. The same formatting changes may be possible in OpenOffice or Pages, but the resulting document may not convert as expected. When using another word processor, be sure to save the file as a Word DOC file. (Some programs use "export" to make this conversion.)

Kindle Direct Publishing will accept a DOC or DOCX file. To save with other programs, follow the tips below.

- OpenOffice

  Use the Save As command and select one of the Microsoft Word file format.

- Pages from Apple

  Use the Export command in the File menu. Select Word then Save.

Kindle accepts PDF files. Textbook Creator and the new Kindle Create use PDF files to produce print replica or fixed layout e-books. More on this in Chapter 9. However, PDF files cause issues with some of the standard Kindle conversion processes. In fact, before upload KDP has a warning screen advising using another file format.

If the manuscript is in PDF format, there a few options for the conversion. The first option uses Adobe Reader. The most recent version has an option to convert a file to a Word DOCX file. This option is available free for one use. After that a premium membership is required. The DOCX file can then be saved as a DOC file as described above.

Second is using Adobe Acrobat. Acrobat has an export function to convert PDF files to a DOC file. Select the Export command from the File menu and choose Word. It's very straightforward. If the PDF file has a lot of additional formatting such as page numbers, headers/footers, or sidebars, it may export with all of those features mingled with the general text.

A third option is an internet service **Nitro**. This service will convert various file formats including PDF to Word. A fourteen-day free trial is available.

When writing a manuscript exclusively for an e-book, using the techniques below from the beginning will save some time when it's time to publish.

Cleaning up

Now that we have a Word document, we can start cleaning it up for the conversion process. No matter which e-book format is being used, we need to start with a bare bones document. These steps are the beginning steps and are for a completely formatted manuscript. However, even if no special formatting has been done, some of the steps listed are needed to ensure a clean document. Steps such as removing sidebars or inserting graphics may not be needed for a fiction book. I encourage reading through this steps to be familiar with the entire process before beginning to format.

Let's start with the hardest first: throwing away some of the elements of the manuscript. Hint: Before beginning to make these changes, save the manuscript file with a new name. Accidents happen and it's nice to have the original file to return to.

1. Remove images

   All images need to be removed. We'll discuss how to return the graphics and photos to the document in Chapter 9. For now, remove all graphics and photos. I recommend saving them to a separate folder. They'll be easier to find when it's time to add them back into the document.

2. Remove pull quotes

Pull quotes are usually added to long areas of text in a print book for the visual enhancement, something not needed in an e-book. If the quote is something to emphasize, use bold type in the text.

I read a book in which the pull quotes had been changed to italic text. A nice touch, but they landed in the middle of sentences. It took several pages for me to realize what was happening. I learned to skip the italic portions while reading. Again, not an easy reader experience. In many cases, pull quotes can be eliminated.

3. Remove sidebars

Sidebars are a different animal. They usually contain additional information, which enhances understanding of the content or have additional details to add clarity for the reader. The sidebars don't need to be completely jettisoned, though. If the information is important for the reader, consider other ways to handle it. One option is to incorporate the information into the text. Another option is to put the information in an appendix at the end of the document. A third way to include the sidebar is to make a graphic textbox, something we'll look at in Chapter 11 on graphics. Don't throw the material away. Cut and paste it into another document to use later.

4. Remove page numbers

I've already mentioned page numbers aren't necessary, so remove them. This can take some time. If the document is divided into formatting sections, the page numbers will need to be removed from each section.

Windows: The **Header/Footer** menu is found in the **Insert** box on the Home Ribbon.

Mac: The **Header/Footer** menu is under the **View** drop-down menu.

In both operating systems, double clicking on the header or footer in the document will open it for editing.

- Open **Headers/Footers** menu.
- Click on the page number and a box will appear around it.
- Delete the number.

All the page numbers in each formatting section will be deleted. (View the nonprinting characters, the backward P in the toolbar, to show the formatting sections.)

Go through the document following these steps until all of the page numbers are removed.

5. Move footnotes

Now it's time to work with the footnotes. If the footnotes are at the bottom of the pages, they will need to be moved.

They can either be put at the end of each chapter (my preference) or at the end of the book. At this point, it's a matter of copying and pasting them to another page in the document. Don't change the reference numbers in the document yet.

If Word's footnote toolbars has been used to create them, **Convert Footnotes to Endnotes** option can be used.

Once the footnotes have been cleaned up, it's time to remove all other details from the headers and footers. These should be empty throughout the document. Like page numbers, it may be necessary to go through the various formatting sections to remove all the header/footer text.

6. Remove the cover photo.

7. Remove blank pages.

8. Remove all formatting.

   If the manuscript is completely formatted with all the paragraph indents, chapter titles, and page breaks, this step often makes us cringe. All of that formatting needs to be cleared away. (Go, have a good cry; return when you are ready.) As one writer said, creating an e-book is more than converting a document.

   I recommend doing this step with an "unformatted" document as well. Word processors can insert hidden codes; all of those codes need to be stripped away. This is the best way to clear all the formatting. When finished, we are left with a plain vanilla document ready for re-formatting for e-book conversion.

If the manuscript has italics, bold, or other such styles, I recommend highlighting these so they can be easily found later. The clear formatting command doesn't remove the highlights.

Windows

- Select the whole document by pressing **CTRL+A** or just select the portion of the document that needs changed.
- Click the **More** button in the **Styles** portion of the Home tab. (It is located just below the down arrow to the right of the styles.)
- Click **Clear Formatting** on the menu that appears.

Mac

- Select the entire document. Under the **Edit** menu, select **Select All**.
- Go back to the **Edit** menu and select **Clear**. In the fly-out menu, select **Clear Formatting**.

9. If the manuscript is double spaced, change it to single space.

10. A bare bones text document is left. Make a backup of this version.

Hidden Format Code

A manuscript exported from another format may have other hidden formatting code. In this case, after completing the steps above the "nuclear option" may be needed.

1. **To do this,** copy and paste the entire document into a text editor **such as Notepad (Win) or TextEdit (Mac).**

2. Now save the document as a TXT file. A warning may be given that formatting will be lost.

3. Go ahead and click **OK** because this is a time to lose the formatting. This method creates a completely clean file to begin the conversion process. Note: highlights for italic or other styles don't remain in a TXT file. There is no way to keep track of this with the nuclear option.

Catherine Ryan Howard[1], author of *Distress Signals*, put it this way:

> I had to go through my book again but, while I did, I was able to pick out a few more errors, clean up a few sentences and generally improve it a bit. So instead of thinking of it as formatting, I just thought of it as another go-through, another revision.[1]

Basic starting steps

Now we have a clean manuscript document. We can start putting back some of what has been removed. It's natural to be thinking, "Why did I remove it only to start over?" When formatting an e-book, remember "simple" is the keyword. Yes, there are fancy e-books available. These are the coffee table books of the e-book industry. We are preparing to publish a book people want to read, not admire.

Change Fonts

When the format was cleared, especially with the nuclear option, the font may have changed to the word processor's default font. The current font is displayed on the Home Menu Ribbon. As discussed in Chapter 7, Times New Roman is generally recommended for the text and Arial for chapter titles and subheads. 12 pt is the standard font size for an e-book. Other simple serif fonts, such as Cambria or Century Schoolbook, may be used also.

Follow the two steps below to change fonts.

1. Select the entire document. (Use either **CTRL+A** (Win), **CMD+A** (Mac) or **Select All** from the **Edit** menu.)

2. From **Font** menu, scroll to Times New Roman in the dropdown menu, select it. 12 pt is the recommended size for e-books.

Done.

Sidebars

If sidebars have been removed, now is the time to decide what to do with the information. This decision may result in some rewriting of the manuscript.

In addition to the options discussed earlier, some writers place their sidebar material between two horizontal lines in the flowing text. Like this:

While this can separate the extra information from the main document, most people won't skip it. They will continue reading as though it's part of the text. A title of the section may help. If using this method, be sure to make a good transition for the readers who simply keep reading.

For readers using large fonts, this method may result in confusion when the material shows up on another page. Don't forget, the good reader experience makes a good e-book.

A simple horizontal separator can be made by typing three symbols, such as underscores, dashes, or asterisks, then hit enter, as below:

--- --- --- --- --- --- --- --- --- --- --- --- --- --- --- --- --- -- -

Another method is to type the simple symbol and center it:

###

A custom horizontal line can be used. This is how

- Start by selecting **Borders and Shading** from the **Format** drop-down menu.
- Click on **Horizontal Line**. Navigate to the horizontal line file. Click **Insert**.

   Know beforehand where the picture or design is located on the hard drive.

Don't use a paragraph border because it won't change well during document conversion. Be aware, a large or detailed horizontal line image may not convert well.

The final, and hardest, option is to include the sidebar in the same area of the chapter in the form of a graphic text box. The reason I say this is the hardest is because the sidebar needs to be re-created as a graphic. The text box graphic then is inserted as any other graphic will be (see Chapter 11 for details about text boxes).

> ### A Sidebar as a Textbox
>
> The information you provide in a sidebar can be put in a textbox.
>
> One problem with a textbox is the font is not scalable. In other words, it won't become larger or smaller as the user adjusts his settings. If the user attempts to enlarge the box to increase the font size, the text may become fuzzy.
>
> The placement of the sidebar may interfere with the smooth flow of reading. This kind of interruption may be a negative experience for the reader.

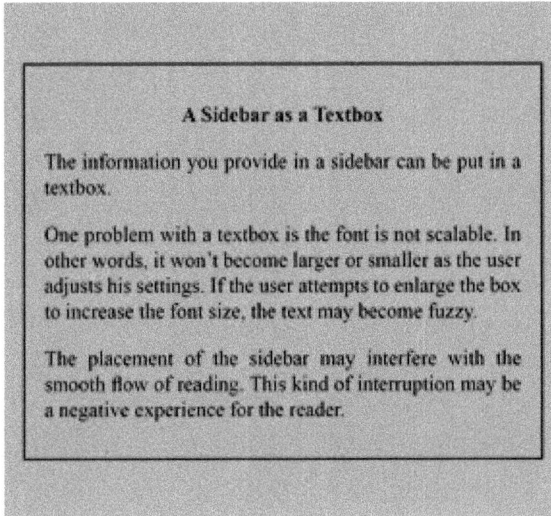

Now we're ready to start more detailed formatting.

Move forward

Check each item as you complete it.

☐ MAKE A BACKUP COPY OF YOUR FILE. (Yes, it's important enough to warrant upper case letters.)

☐ Remove graphics. Save them to another folder first.

☐ Remove pull quotes.

☐ Remove sidebars. Save the material in another document with a different file name in another file folder.

☐ Remove page numbers.

☐ Move footnotes to the end of each chapter or the end of the book.

☐ Remove cover image.

☐ Clear formatting.

☐ If needed, use the nuclear option to clear unseen code.

☐ Change fonts.

☐ If not already completed, re-write sidebars.

Now we're all set to start preparing those manuscripts for e-publishing.

Endnotes

1. Howard, Catherine Ryan, 2011, "Backpacked Weekend: A new and easier way to format your e-book," September 5, 2011, accessed November 8, 2014, http://catherineryanhoward.com/2011/09/05/backpacked-week-a-new-and-improved-even-easier-way-to-format-your-e-book/

CHAPTER NINE

NEXT FORMATTING STEPS

Now that some of the document's elements that aren't needed in most e-books have been removed, let's move on to the formatting process. At this point the document may include everything except a cover: the title page, copyright page, table of contents, content, and back matter. If the title page, copyright page, or table of contents haven't been created, wait until we have some of the formatting completed.

These instructions generally apply to both Kindle and EPUB files. Some of the aggregators and distributors may have some slight variations in handling such things as table of contents. Be sure to check their style guide.

Inserting page breaks

What is an e-page?

An e-book doesn't have pages. It appears to have pages when we read on a device, but in fact, it's one long document. When we can change the font size, the "pages" will be different.

There are two schools of thought about handling page breaks. One says to leave page breaks after each chapter and each of the front matter pages. Not surprisingly, the other school says not to use page breaks.

Some manuals recommend placing four line spaces between sections and chapters. The problem I've seen with this method is when the reader is using a large font size; the space between chapters may be too large and leave blank pages. I recommend using page breaks.

If the nuclear option was used to remove extra formatting, page breaks will be removed. If the nuclear blast isn't needed, the page breaks will be fine.

It's possible some page breaks aren't appropriate for a specific e-book. They can be easily removed.

1. Select the **Show All Nonprinting Character** button at the top of the screen. It looks like a backward P.

2. Go through the document, select the page break character (usually appears as line with the words "page break") and delete.

Now the small details

It's time to go back and put in the fine formatting details—bold, italic, block quotes. Yes, once again it's a tedious process. One that leave us wondering whether it's worth going to all of trouble to remove formatting if we're only going to put it back in.

Yes, it is, in order to produce a quality product. It's amazing what might be hidden that can cause a problem during conversion. When extra spaces between paragraphs or odd symbols show up in an e-book, someone hasn't gone to this type of detail in creating the product. Quite honestly, if it isn't done now, we end up mucking through the document after conversion to try and find what is causing the problem.

When planning to also convert the book to EPUB format, use styles to add bold, italic, and other styles. It will make the conversion easier.

Paragraphs

A general formatting rule is nonfiction uses no indent and has space between paragraphs. And fiction uses paragraph indentation and no paragraph spaces. Of course, it's your book; choose how you want it to look.

If using indents at the beginning of the paragraphs, styles will once again make the task easier.

1. Select all of the text in the section that is to have a paragraph indent. This is commonly between sub-heads.

2. From the **Styles** menu, select **Body Text First Indent**. The style may be modified to make the indent larger or smaller and remove spacing between the paragraphs. Again, the style can be renamed for this use.

Don't use tabs or spaces to create indents. This can cause funny spacing in the content when the reader changes the text size.

Where a block-style paragraph, like this book, is used, instead of using a hard return between paragraphs, set "paragraph spacing."

If hard returns (or two carriage returns) have already been used between paragraphs, they need to be removed. I found it easier to remove them one section at time before moving on to the next step, rather than trying to do the whole document. Don't use **Find and Replace** to remove the carriage returns. Chapter title and sub-heading formatting may be inadvertently be removed at the same time.

1. Select the section where added line spacing is needed.

2. Select paragraph from the **Format** menu.

3. In the **Indent and Spacing** tab, in the spacing section set the **After** space to the space desired. (This document uses 6 pt) Set the line spacing to **Single**.

Although this can be tedious, once a flow is established, it will move right along well.

Preparing the table of contents

The TOC will consist of chapter titles, sub-heads if desired, but no page numbers. Remember page numbers are irrelevant in an e-book. Some instructions recommend keeping the chapter headings as simply "Chapter 1," "Chapter 2," "Chapter 3," and so on. For a good preview give the chapters clear titles. The TOC is one more way to let potential buyers know what the book is about. Like the book title, avoid "cute" chapter titles. Be clear so readers can easily see what the book is about. For fiction, using a TOC with numbered chapter titles may make navigation through the book easier.

Chapter Titles

Whether chapter titles or only number designators are used, they need to be formatted correctly so the TOC is easier to build.

For this section, a little knowledge about styles is needed. To learn more about Word styles, tutorials are found in the Resource appendix.

Chapter titles need to be in a style named Heading 1; it is a built-in style. This is one of the common styles located in the Styles box on the Home Menu Ribbon on both PCs and Macs.

1. Highlight the text of the chapter title.

2. Scroll through the **Styles** to find **Heading 1**.

3. Select **Heading 1** from the Styles list.

4. Click on the **Heading 1** style.

    Keyboard commands can be used to apply the Heading 1 style.

    1. Highlight the chapter title text to be used

    2. Use the following commands

        Windows: CTRL + ALT + 1

        Mac: CMD + OPT +1

NOTE: Heading 1 uses the default font in 16 pt. This can be changed by

1. Selecting Heading 1 in the Styles list.

2. Selecting **Modify** to make changes.

Chapter titles can be formatted for any look that fits with the content, including alignment on the page. Again, I recommend sticking with a standard sans serif font, such as Arial or Helvetica.

Go through the document repeating the steps above until all the chapter titles have been formatted. The same style can be used for the back matter sections as well. We'll build the table of contents after all the formatting is completed.

Sub-Titles

Sometimes sub-titles are included in the TOC. To add sub-titles, follow the steps above using **Heading 2**. Again, the Heading 2 style can be modified. When styles are added the sub-titles may look orphaned. Don't worry it won't show up in the final document.

Building the table of contents

Amazon instructions recommend that Windows users generate the table of contents using **Word's built-in table of contents creator**. Mark Coker of Smashwords and others in the industry recommend against using this method because the TOC creator adds code that might not be needed. The recommended method is to manually build the TOC using bookmarks and hyperlinks.

The TOC list can be created without typing in each item. This is where Word's built-in Table of Contents tool can be used. Generally, the TOC will be after the copyright page.

1. Add a page break after the copyright page to make a page for the TOC.

2. Type "Table of Contents," and format it to match chapter titles. Press Enter.

3. Use the **Index and Tables** menu.

Windows:

1. Open the **References** tab in the navigation ribbon.

2. Find **Table of Contents** and click on it. Select **Insert Table of Contents**.

3. Uncheck the box that says **Show page numbers**.

4. In the **Show Levels** box, choose 1 if the sub-titles aren't included in the TOC. Choose 2 if they are.

5. Click **OK.**

There's a selection **Use hyperlinks instead of page numbers**. To manually create the chapter links do not select this option.

Mac:

The **Index and Tables** menu is under the **Insert** menu.

1. Find the **Table of Contents** tab and click on it.

2. Select a format from the list. A sample of each format can be viewed in the box to the left.

3. Uncheck the box that says **Show page numbers**.

4. Click **OK**

A page with the table of content listings is automatically created.

Bookmarks

Mac users can skip to Link the Table of Contents below. The chapter and subhead bookmarks will be inserted during the creation of the table of contents.

Windows:

To manually build the TOC, each chapter title and sub-title needs to be bookmarked.

The first step is to bookmark each chapter title.

1. On the beginning page of each chapter, highlight the chapter title. The chapter number (if used), the title of the chapter, or both can be highlighted.

2. Click on the **Bookmark** item in the **Insert** menu.

3. Give the chapter bookmark a name. I like to use numbers in the bookmark names, such as "chp1," "chp2," and so on. When it's time to create the TOC links, the chapter

bookmarks will be in the order in which they'll be used. Please note, the number is not in front and there are no spaces in the bookmark. As the bookmarks are created, they are added to the bookmark list.

Follow the same procedure for the subheads, using a naming scheme to help find the bookmark when it is needed.

The hard work of creating the table of contents completed. It's time to build it.

Linking the Table of Contents

Now the chapter bookmarks need to be hyperlinked to the TOC created earlier.

1. Highlight the chapter name in the table of contents.

2. Select **Hyperlink** from the **Insert** menu or use the keyboard option CTRL+K (Win), CMD+K (Mac).

3. Select **Document** from the middle of the dialog box.

4. Find the bookmark name in the **Bookmark** list in the center box..

5. Select the chapter bookmark and click **OK.**

An EPUB table of contents is created differently than Kindle. The bookmark/hyperlink method will help with both. I have had no TOC problems by doing it manually.

For both systems:

The Kindle system needs to know where to find the TOC. So place a bookmark named "toc" (without the quotes) on the words "Table of Contents."

Move forward

☐ Check the page breaks.

☐ Set the paragraph spacing, if needed. (Most fiction titles indent paragraphs, leaving no space between them.)

☐ Format chapter titles using styles to create H1 titles. If you will be adding subheads to the TOC, format these with H2.

☐ Prepare and create the table of contents.

You'll be glad you paid attention to the details.

CHAPTER TEN

FINAL FORMATTING DETAILS

Front matter

The front matter, title page, copyright page, and preface, are in place. As mentioned previously, an e-book will have fewer pages in the front. The usual acknowledgments, dedication, and endorsements should be moved to the back of the book.

As part of the publishing process, Amazon creates a preview for all Kindle books. The preview is about 10 percent of the book. People want to see the actual content, not endorsements and acknowledgments. The title page, copyright, and table of contents are important front matter in the preview, although some e-book formatters are recommending the TOC be moved to the back of the book as well. Personally, I like to review the table of contents before purchasing a nonfiction book. Make it possible for previewers to see as much content as possible. Start with the title page and count to see about where the preview will end.

Set up the title page and copyright page the same as for a print edition. We still want to use standard fonts for e-publications, even if something fancier was used in the print or PDF versions. Be sure to use a page break after each of these pages so they will be on separate pages in the e-book. Some writers who don't have an ISBN or a LOC number for their e-books, are putting copyright information on the title page.

Footnotes

Footnotes should now be endnotes, either at the end of the chapters or the end of the book. While a link from the note reference to the note itself isn't necessary, readers now want more interactivity, so we want to consider doing it. Yes, it's another detail that takes time, but it creates a better product.

To hyperlink endnotes:

1. Create a bookmark for each note. Use the same method as used for the TOC.

2. When naming the bookmark, make it something easy to remember and find later. I use a naming scheme to allow me to know what it is (a reference), the chapter number, and note number. So the bookmark name looks like "ref_1_1." This also places the bookmarks in numerical

order for ease in linking. The bookmark name can't have any spaces in it.

3. Now, go to each reference number and create a hyperlink. Follow same the instructions for creating hyperlinks in the TOC instructions.

A hyperlink for each endnote can also be created so the reader can easily return to the referring page. Generally, a link is added to the note number. Some only add one link on the endnote page, which returns to the beginning of the chapter. Again this can be a tedious process, but it adds to the reading experience.

Create links to other chapters by creating internal links using the same process outlined above. The same instructions can be used if an index is added to the book.

Website URLs

After creating hyperlinks for the endnotes, creating URL hyperlinks will be a breeze.

Use the same process as creating a bookmark.

1. Highlight the words that to link to a website.

2. Select **Hyperlink** from the **Insert** menu.

3. Select **Web Page**. This is generally the default selection.

4. In the **Link to** box, type in the URL, including "http://"

5. The words highlighted in step one should already be in the **Display** box. If not, type them in now.

6. Click **OK**.

It's easy to mistype a long, complicated URL. To make it easier, while I'm formatting my books, I put the entire URL, offset by brackets, in the text where I want it. (I use copy and paste from my web browser.) Then I can copy the URL to paste into the **Link to** box. Finally, I delete the URL from the text. This may sound like extra work, but it's easier than trying to figure out which little character was left out of the URL.

A word about affiliate links: Kindle does not allow affiliate links in e-books, not even Amazon affiliate links.

Move Forward

☐ Add the front matter.

☐ Create endnote links.

Congratulations! A lot of the hard details are now completed.

You are now ready to add the special details.

CHAPTER ELEVEN

GRAPHICS, TEXT BOXES, COVERS

E-readers weren't originally designed for graphics and photographs. Text is still the foundation, but as the technology improves, e-books have changed. Now even graphic-heavy children's books and "coffee-table" books are possible. It is important to remember some readers may be using an older device, which may not handle graphics well.

Older e-devices, especially older Kindles, will allow graphics to rotate but lack the ability to zoom and pan as the newer devices and apps do. This is especially important for tables and text boxes.

Images

An image can be a photograph, a text box, or line art. All of these are handled generally in the same way, but there are some specific details for each one. For complete details of formatting and using images, I highly recommend *Pictures on Kindle* by Aaron Shepard.

Generally, images are rendered on a full page (more on having text and images on the same page later). Although it's possible to have text surrounding an image, it requires HTML programming skills. Programming code is beyond the scope of this book.

Some things to take into account:

Image Size

There are three aspects to image size: the dimensions of the image, image quality, and the file size.

- Dimensions. Because the image will use a separate page in the e-book, it's recommended the image be 600 pixels (px) wide and 800 px tall. (Nook image size is limited to 730 px wide.) This size works across most of the legacy devices as well as mobile devices. If the original image is smaller, quality will be lost as it is made larger.

- Image Quality (Resolution). This is usually designated as dots per inch (dpi). While a 300 dpi or higher image is better for printing, a smaller dpi is better for electronics. A 72-dpi image works well for all devices.

- File size. This is the size of the image file. This information is in the file details in Explorer (Win) or Finder (Mac). 5MB is the largest image file size for Kindle.

File Format

Most e-book conversions allow the following file formats: GIF, JPG (sometimes listed as JPEG). PNG, BMP, and SVG. I have found JPG most universal. JPG files are also smaller than the others. Kindle recommends JPG for photos and GIF for line drawings. Kindle has some specifics on when to use other file formats in their **Publishing Guidelines**.

(Note: Sometimes a photo or graphic has .jpeg as the file extender. I always change the file name so the extender is .jpg because some services don't recognize the four-letter extender. They are both the same file format.)

Graphic Tweaking

Word processors are just that—they work with words, not graphics. Most word processors have simple graphic editing tools, but they don't really manipulate the images in the same way a graphic program does. Do all of the tweaking of size, color, cropping, etc. in a graphic program. The only thing that should be done within the word processor is page placement. If the graphic doesn't look right or doesn't fit, take it back to the graphics program, make the adjustments, and then re-insert in the document.

Graphics and photos may be rendered in greyscale (in multiple shades of grey, such as photos in a newspaper) on older devices. A highly detailed graphic or a photo with subtle shadings may not appear as clear as in color.

To view a graphic in greyscale using Word:

1. Open a new document and insert the image.

2. Under the **Format** menu select **Picture**.

3. In the option box, find **Adjust Picture**. Select **Greyscale**.

Word 2016:

Follow instructions 1 and 2 above.

1. Select **Picture Format** ribbon in the top menu.

2. Select **Color**.

3. In the **Recolor** section, make a greyscale selection. There are several.

(Graphics program such as Paint (Windows), Paintbrush (Mac), Photoshop, or **Gimp,** a free program, will do most of the changes needed).

Text Boxes

As mentioned in previous chapters, considering the way e-readers render the material, it's best to not have pull-quotes or sidebars as they are used in print books. It is, however, possible to create a text box graphic for this information. A standard text box in a word processor will do strange things to all of the text, including not even showing up in some devices.

It's possible to create a text box graphic using a graphics program such as Photoshop or Gimp, but some e-readers may not like them. A text graphic with more than a couple lines of text may be resized by the e-reader causing it to blur. Preview before publishing to be sure the graphic renders correctly.

Graphic programs have specific tools for creating a text box graphic. In general, start a new image, set the size for the image (no larger than 600 px horizontally for a full-page image for most devices), and use the Text Tool to write the text in the box. I recommend adding a border to the box so it can be distinguished from the body text. Save the text image as a JPG, GIF, or PNG. Follow the same guidelines for an image graphic above.

When creating a text box image, consider changing to a different font to further set off the text. Remember, fancy fonts will not be readable on older devices, even in a text box. Don't use background shading for any portion of this text area. Older e-readers will see those areas as black.

It's beyond the scope of this book to go into the details of creating text box graphics. I used Adobe Illustrator for the text boxes for this book. The free image program Gimp also has tools to make a text box. Once the graphic is created, it will be inserted into the e-book file the same way as other images.

Tables

Many books have tables to illustrate points. If the table is inserted as a Word-created table, it may break across pages, drop columns, or place the columns on different pages. A table should be converted to a graphic.

Before beginning to create a table, be sure it's in portrait orientation and is longer than is wider. Keep in mind how an e-book places graphics on the page. The information may need to be split into two tables to accommodate all the details. Otherwise the text in the table may become too small to read without zooming the graphic.

A landscape-oriented table will force the reader to try to turn the e-book. Many e-readers automatically rotate the screen. This will force readers to change the e-reader settings to turn off screen rotation or to tilt their head to see the information.

1. Use a new document to make the table.

2. Create the table using the Word table tools found in the **Table** menu.

3. When the table is created and formatted, select the entire table.

4. Copy the table into a favorite graphic program.

5. Save as a JPG file (.jpg).

The table can now be inserted following the instructions below for inserting images. Melinda Martin of Martin Publishing Services recommends a table graphic had 300 dpi resolution. She says the details of the text and numbers in the table will be clearer.

Text with Graphics

To add a caption or other text to an image, put it directly on the photo or graphic. Then insert the entire graphic into the DOC file. Here's a sample of photos and text on the same page.

The Dog
The dog is a friend and companion

Dogs have held notable positions as Not only companions, but also servants that performed countless duties and tasks such as beasts of burden and sentries. They were mates and unfortunately even Food!

Cats, on the other hand, are lazy good-for-nothing slackers that contribute noth-ing to society. They Do contribute to aler gies!

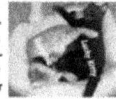

(Photo from **https://kdp.amazon. com/community/thread. jspa?messageID=573716&** — 573716, no longer available)

Children's books are often made up entirely of graphics so the text and pictures are on the same page. Each page in the book **Out and About at the Zoo** is a graphic.

Kindle now has a tool for **creating children's books.**

File Storage

I recommend keeping graphic files in a separate file folder for easier access as they are manipulated and added to the DOC file. Numbering the file name in the order it is to be placed in the manuscript, such as 1graphic.jpg, 2chart.jpg, 2textbox.jpg, makes the task easier.

Inserting images

Each graphic should be one separate page and should fill the page. The dimensions given above fill an e-page.

1. Find the text where the graphic is to be located. Place the cursor there.

2. Under the **Insert** menu, select **Photo,** followed by **Picture from File**. The graphic may be a drawing, but the file format will be recognized with this selection. If the graphics have already been placed in a separate folder, they'll be easy to find.

Word 2016: Select **Pictures** in the **Insert** menu. Then select **Picture from File**. Note: **Pictures in File** can only be selected when using a DOCX file.

1. Locate the graphic file and insert it into the document.

2. The only adjustment that should be made is to anchor the graphic so it doesn't float around with the text. Highlight

the graphic. Select **Picture** from the **Format** menu. In the **Layout** section select **In Line with Text**.

Word 2016: Select the **Layout** ribbon. Select **Position**. **In Line** is the default setting, however double check to be sure.

Caution: Do not copy and paste the graphic into the document. It needs to be embedded as a file.

To avoid extra space or "pages" before and after an image, Aaron Shepard recommends adding a paragraph page break. This is not the same page break we normally use to create a new page.

Here's how to find the paragraph page break:

Windows

Use the **Paragraph** section in the Home Menu Ribbon.

Mac

Click on **Format** in the top menu bar, then click on **Paragraph**.

For both platforms, use the following instructions:

1. Select the image.

Word 2016: Place the cursor in the line before the image. Don't select the image.

1. Go to the **Paragraph** formatting section.

2. Click **Line and Page** breaks.

3. Select **Page break before**.

Fixed-layout books

It now easier to have a fixed-layout book. Fixed-layout books are generally graphic-heavy, such as children's books, graphic novels, and photography books. KDP has special tools to format and convert these manuscripts (see Chapter 4). Using these tools, it's possible to have a Kindle book with the same layout as the print edition. One caveat with fixed-layout books is the reader is unable to resize the text or use other user controls. Most devices allow the reader to zoom in and out, but that's not quite the same.

Covers

We've discussed the importance of a good cover, whether for a print book or an e-book. The e-book cover is uploaded as a separate file. It's used on the product page as well as on the e-book. The cover is also displayed on the e-reading device. But it isn't necessary to include the cover in the e-book manuscript file.

There are a few formatting differences for a cover.

- Image Dimensions. The cover image, a JPG or TIF file, is larger than the graphics inside the e-book. The minimum size for Kindle (which also can be used for other e-readers) is 1000 px on the longest side and 650 px on the shortest side. KDP recommends 4500 px tall and 2820 px wide for highest quality. Kindle recommends a 1.6:1 height/width ratio. So at minimum, the cover size recommended is 1000 px by 1600 px; maximum 2500 px by 1562 px. The cover image should be formatted for 72 dpi and the file no larger than 50 MB.

This is information a graphic designer will need to produce a quality cover.

- Placement of Cover Image. Create a separate file for the cover image. Do not include it in the manuscript document. Most e-book conversions add the cover automatically during the process.

- Color. The image should use RGB color mode. This is the mode used by electronics. A print color image is usually CMYK (four color image process). This image can be converted to RGB using a graphics program.

- Greyscale Cover Image. I've read recommendations of adding a greyscale image of the cover at the beginning of the manuscript document as an inside graphic. This is to help those with legacy e-readers to see the cover. It's purely an option. Remember, this optional inside cover will take one page of the preview sample.

One Small Detail

While most formatting options, such as underline or strikethrough, translate well during the conversion, symbols may not.

Symbols are anything added using **Symbols** or **Advanced Symbols** in the **Insert** menu. It's recommended for common symbols such as ©, to use words. Mark Coker of Smashwords put it this way, "If it can't be made using the keyboard, it probably won't work."

Even if graphics aren't planned for the current work-in-progress, it's a good idea to practice using the tools. When the time comes to add graphics to a later project, you'll be prepared.

For a detailed and technical discussion of these topics, download **Amazon Kindle Publishing Guidelines.**

Move Forward

☐ If you are using images, text boxes, or tables, prepare and insert them into your file.

☐ Add your cover image.

We are ready to publish.

CHAPTER TWELVE

PUBLISHING YOUR E-BOOK

The manuscript, cover, and graphics (if any) are now ready for conversion. Kindle Digital Publishing (KDP) is the most popular publishing option for do-it-yourself individuals, which is why we'll use the Amazon Kindle system to convert the documents. It's possible to practice using the system. Unless the "Publish Your Kindle Book" button is pushed, it won't go into the Amazon system. (Even if the practice file is "published" accidently, it can be removed.)

While the basic principles are the same, each company has different requirements for uploading. Be sure to read the specific instructions if using a different e-publishing company. Amazon is making many changes right now, so be sure to check for updates to this information. (Changes are published on the Formatting e-Books Facebook group.) Most companies accept DOC, MOBI, or EPUB.

KDP now accepts files in a variety of formats, except MOBI files created with Mobipocket Creator. KDP offers **KindleGen** to create MOBI files. There are so many other options, however, I see no reason to use a MOBI file.

File type

KDP now accepts files in the following formats: DOC, DOCX, HTML, MOBI, EPUB, RTF, TXT, PDF, KPF (Kindle Package Format). However, each file type has some quirks. Some of the issues to watch out for:

- DOC, DOCX, RTF files should only be used for manuscripts without complex formatting.

- MOBI is the foundation format for Kindle's AZW file. As a reminder, Kindle doesn't support MOBI files created with Mobipocket Creator. Most files can be converted to MOBI using Calibre.

- TXT files are the barest of files with little or no formatting options.

- PDF files carry over special formatting, which may cause problems with a Kindle conversion. KDP doesn't recommend this file format except for fixed format books.

- EPUB files have greater formatting options, but KDP still recommends testing with Kindle Previewer or Kindle Gen. Converting to a MOBI file with Calibre may also show any problems that could come up with an EPUB file. Many writers choose EPUB files because programs such as Scrivner and Apple Pages have good conversion options.

- HTML files are the most reliable because they more closely resemble the "language" AZW speaks. KDP gives instructions for HTML files in their documentation.

By far the best file type for any e-book conversion is HTML. Because an e-book is like one long web page, an HTML (the basic web page language) file is the purest format for any e-book. For those who are comfortable with HTML code, KindleGen will help with the process. Never fear. It isn't necessary to learn HTML programming, though. Thus, the instructions below are to create a HTML file.

Prepare the HTML file

Preparing an HTML file for uploading is a matter of how the document is saved. We will be working from a Word DOC/DOCX. It's also highly recommended a PDF file be converted to DOC/DOCX. A word of caution: Review the file converted from PDF for formatting problems. I highly recommend if a PDF file has been converted to a DOC file, go back through the manuscript from the beginning of the formatting process.

The first step is saving all of the book files so they are easy to find during the process. Put all of the e-book files in a new folder: cover file, manuscript file, and graphics files. These should be copies of the original files. Be sure to have these files backed up, just in case. I also recommend giving these files new names to avoid confusion.

Conversion step one—HTML

Depending on the version of Word being used, the **File** menu may be an option to **Save As Web Page** ... If this option is available, use it. If not, use the **Save As** option under the **File** menu.

To use the "Save As" option:

In the dialog box, a drop-down menu is in the center of the box. This is a menu item most of us don't notice when we're saving files.

Using the instructions below, save the new file in the folder just created for the conversion files.

Windows

1. In the drop-down menu, select **Web Page, Filtered**.

2. Click **Save**. If prompted with a warning "removing office tags," click **yes**.

Mac:

1. In the drop-down menu, select **Web Page (htm).**

2. In the bottom half of the dialog box, find the **Save only display information into HTML**. Check the button in front of this option.

3. Click **Save**.

Note: Recent versions of Word for Mac have a **Save as Web Page** option in the **File** menu. The same instructions apply.

An HTML file is now created.

Conversion step two—Graphic files

If there are no photos or graphics in the manuscript, it isn't necessary to create the ZIP files described below. Again, consider practicing to gain experience with ZIP files.

Manuscripts with image files need a ZIP file of the files and folders. The graphic files are handled a little differently for Windows and Mac.

Navigate to the new folder with the files. There should be an HTML file (or it may be labeled HTM) and a folder with the same name as the manuscript files. This folder was created when the original file was converted to HTML.

Windows:

1. Right click on the HTML file in the Explorer listing.

2. Scroll over to **Send to** on the menu, click **Compressed (zipped) folder**. A new folder with a zipper on it will appear.

3. Drag the images folder onto the new zipped file.

Change the name of the new zipped folder to avoid confusion.

Mac:

1. Click on the manuscript file to highlight it.

2. Hold down the **Command** key and click on the folder with the same name as the manuscript file. Both the file and the folder should be highlighted now.

    It should look something like this:

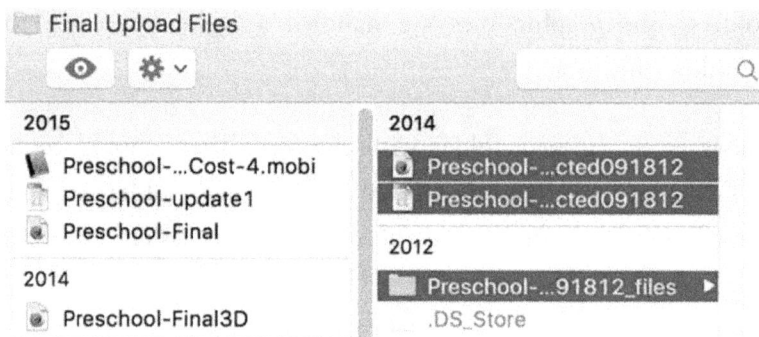

3. Right click on one of the highlighted names.

4. Select **Compress 2 items** from the drop-down menu.

This will create a folder named "Archive.zip." I recommend changing the name of this folder to the name of the e-book.

File Upload

The files should now be ready to upload for conversion to a Kindle product: cover, manuscript in HTML, and a zip folder.

As I said before, the files can be uploaded to KDP for practice using the system to create a Kindle product. The book will not be published until the system is told to publish. In addition to getting a feel for the publishing process and some of the questions that need to be answered, the practice also gives an opportunity to view the manuscript as a Kindle e-book.

Conversion to a MOBI file, which can be used on a Kindle, can be done with Calibre but may not look exactly like it will on a Kindle.

Your KDP account should already be set up. If not, do it now. Instructions are in Appendix 3.

Uploading your book

Once the publishing account is set up, the Bookshelf will have **Create A New Title** at the top with the selection of previously published titles, if any, below. Select **Kindle eBook** from Create a New Title. This will open to a page with three tabs: Kindle eBook Details, Kindle eBook Content, Kindle eBook Pricing. The first tab, Kindle eBook Details, is opened.

Language

> Select the language of the e-book.

Book Title

> Enter the book title. A subtitle is optional

Series (optional)

Edition Number (optional)

> This can be used when a book has had a significant update.

Author

> The primary author is listed here.

Contributors (optional)

> Editors, illustrators, and other contributors to the publication can be added here. There is a drop-down list to choose from.

Description

This is the book description, which is seen on the Amazon product detail page. It can be up to 4,000 characters.

Publishing Rights

Select the appropriate option.

Keywords

Up to seven keywords can be added.

Categories

KDP allows two categories.

Age and Grade Range (optional)

Used for children's books.

Pre-order (optional)

KDP now allows a book to be offered for pre-order up to ninety days before its release date. To take advantage of this option, a draft manuscript must be uploaded. Amazon will set up a product detail page for the book. Customers can purchase the title anytime leading up to the release date. It will automatically be sent to the buyer on the release date. KDP penalizes the publisher if the pre-release date is missed. I recommend having the draft file as complete as possible to avoid possible delays in the release.

At the end of this page, select "Save as Draft" to return to the publishing process later, or select "Save and Continue."

The next tab, Kindle eBook Content, is used to upload the manuscript file for conversion.

Manuscript

Digital Rights Management (DRM) – Select "Yes" to enable DRM or "No" to refuse DRM.

After the DRM selection, click the "Upload ebook manuscript" button to locate the necessary files and begin uploading. When the upload is complete, a notice will be given as to whether it is successful or not. KDP also notes any possible spelling errors. This can be checked when previewing the converted file.

Kindle eBook Cover

Select the Cover Creator or Upload a cover file.

Kindle eBook Preview

Now it's time to preview the converted book. This is when little glitches may be found. Sometimes the hiccups may be a simple formatting problem or they may be more serious, like a graphic showing up in the wrong place.

When I published my first Kindle book, I had thirteen versions before I liked what I produced. Most of these changes were my own preferences; such as I didn't like the way the subheads looked.

The preveiwer has several options to view the book as though reading on the various Kindle devices, tablets, or phones.

Online Previewer

This is a quick and easy way to see how the e-book will look on various devices.

Download Book Preview File

I recommend downloading this file, even if not previewing on a computer or e-reading device. This download is a MOBI file that can be sent to reviewers or sold from a website. If the file is downloaded, it can be transferred to an e-reader or viewed on a computer. (Note: the new Kindle Create files do not allow this option. More information about Kindle Create is in Chapter 4.)

Download Previewer

This is simply a way to view the book as it will look on a Kindle. I didn't like using it and opted to use my downloaded file with the Kindle app on my computer. **Get a reading app here.**

Aaron Shepard has **a complete article on various ways to preview** and test the Kindle book. Shepard mentions Kindle

Previewer 3 in the introduction. Previewer 3 was released in the fall of 2017. **Here's the details**.

Kindle eBook ISBN (optional)

ISBN (optional)

A Kindle book is not required to have an ISBN. If one is desired, the publisher/writer needs to purchase it.

Publisher's Name (optional)

Many writers choosing to self-publish will create an imprint.

Again, the option to "Save as Draft" or "Save and Continue" is at the bottom of the page.

The next tab, Kindle eBook Pricing, is the last page before publishing. (Although we'll go through the steps, the document won't be published.)

KDP Select Enrollment (optional)

Territories

Territories for which the writer holds distribution rights are selected. For most self-published books, this will be All Territories or worldwide rights.

Royalty and Pricing

KDP Pricing Support

This is a new feature for KDP to help publishers determine optimal price for the e-book. (See Chapter 4 for details.)

Select a royalty plan

E-books priced between 99 cents and $9.99 are eligible for 70% royalty. All others are eligible for 35% royalty. KDP sets a minimum price based on the size of the file. Books with many photos will have a higher minimum than one that is text only.

Primary Marketplace

Amazon.com is generally the primary marketplace. Other marketplaces will be included. The price in the other marketplaces will be calculated automatically based on the Amazon.com price. Some international markets have only a 35% royalty.

Matchbook (optional)

This option is only available for Kindle books that are also sold as print books and gives customers an option to purchase a Kindle book for a reduced price when a print edition is bought.

Book Lending (optional)

This option allows book purchasers to lend the e-book for up to fourteen days. Although listed as optional, all e-books in the 70% royalty program are enrolled in the program.

(More information on Matchbook and Book Lending are in Chapter 4)

Terms & Conditions

KDPs terms and conditions can be found by clicking the link.

When this page is finished, the option is to "Save as Draft" or "Publish Your Kindle eBook."

Correcting problems

After previewing the e-book, some problems with the formatting or text, large or small, may need to be fixed. Corrections can be made in the HTML file and uploaded again. I recommend only those who are familiar with basic HTML programming language try this. It's easy to mess up a programming instruction without even trying.

I advise writers to make changes in the Word document and saving again as a new HTML file. This does take a little longer, but I think it creates fewer problems. I always save as version 2, version 3, and so on. This way if I need to go back to review what I've done, it's easy to find the changes. Make only one change at a time. We never know what the change may do. If several are made at one time, it may be impossible to know which one is causing further problems.

After making corrections, go back to the **Bookshelf**. Here are the steps for uploading a corrected file:

1. On the right of the box for the book needing correction, click on the box with three dots. This will open a drop-down menu.

2. Select **Edit eBook Contents**. This opens to the **Kindle eBook Content** tab.

3. Upload the corrected file in the **Manuscript** box by selecting the **Browse** button.

4. After uploading the new file, scroll to the bottom of the page and select "Save and Continue."

   I recommend previewing the new file before proceeding.

5. If there are no changes on the **Kindle eBook Pricing** page, scroll to the bottom of the page and click **Publish Your Kindle eBook**.

The process of corrections can be done as many times as necessary to get the product just right.

Go to Chapter 13 for more help with Kindle problems and troubleshooting tips.

If the file has been uploaded as a practice exercise, sign out now. I recommend signing in again, go to the bookshelf, and delete the practice file.

If a file to be published is uploaded, click "Save As Draft." Doing so will allow the converted file to simmer a day, then go back and thoroughly go through the preview for any problems. It's easy to return to the bookshelf and complete the publishing process later.

Problems after publishing

After I published my Kindle book, I realized I had somehow left out the title page. Problems can be corrected or content added or removed by uploading a new file. Go to the Bookshelf and follow the steps above for uploading a new file.

It isn't necessary to re-enter information or upload the cover again. Just upload the new manuscript file, preview, and proceed to Save and Continue.

KDP will automatically notify owners of previously purchased Kindle books for serious updates. Serious updates mean "the new version corrects problems that made the book very difficult to read." However, the writer needs to notify KDP to notify purchasers. Here's a link to KDP's instructions: http://amzn.to/2nbfeDz

Congratulations! You've converted and uploaded an e-book!

With a few minor changes, other distributors use similar procedures for converting an e-book to the proper format for other companies. Instructions for other formats are in the appendix. When using an aggregator or company, check their website for specific publishing instructions.

Move Forward

☐ If you haven't already done so, set up your Kindle Direct Publishing account.

☐ Prepare your file for upload following the instructions to change to HTML file.

☐ Upload your file to KDP.

☐ Preview your book using the KDP previewer. If you have an e-reader device, preview your e-book with it.

☐ Correct any problems that may have shown up.

☐ Publish!

Whew! You made it. Now take a break and celebrate.

CHAPTER THIRTEEN

TROUBLESHOOTING

IT'S A RAINY SUNDAY AFTERNOON and I'm sitting in a cafe in central Tokyo, desperately trying to enjoy a book on my iPad. Distractions abound: *sloppy typography, misspelled words, confusing page breaks, widows, orphans, broken tables.* These and more pull me from the narrative spell. In that moment I realize, although I've had this substantial object of glass and metal for a few weeks, I haven't managed more than ten pages of anything. ~~Craig Mod[1]

This comment was written in 2010 (yes, a lifetime away in electronic life), and Mr. Mod's article was about the problems with e-reading devices at the time. Take a look at the words in italic (in original). Those are still distractions in e-books and are all problems that can be taken care of before publishing any book, print or electronic.

It may be time consuming to look for the small details that show up in an e-book, but it's worth the effort to have a quality product offering a good reader experience. Some people purchase an e-book before purchasing the print edition (this is why I recommend both). I noticed readers who purchased my e-book often later had bought the print version. If an e-book is problem-laden, print sales will suffer.

Test, test, test

It's possible to test an e-book in multiple platforms. For those who have an e-reader, I highly recommend using it for the first preview. This is what the reader will see. Various previewers can be downloaded to a computer or tablet to get an idea of how it will look under different conditions.

Use KDP's previewer in the publishing area. Be sure to look at the product in all the versions available. The online previewer gives an idea of what the e-book will look like on various devices and with various font sizes. The device drop-down menu is on the right of the screen and the font size is on the left. This will show any major and minor problems.

Test the e-book, not just on various readers, but also in different font sizes. Changing the font size shouldn't change the formatting. Having font larger than 14 pt is one of the problem areas. Another is too many carriage returns between lines and paragraphs, not to mention huge graphics.

Be sure to look at the e-book in landscape mode as well as portrait. Some devices render landscape as a two-page spread, others as one wider page. Both of these situations can cause unanticipated problems, such as an image stretching out of shape. Never assume how the reader will look at an e-book.

More eyes

Many writers use beta readers to find out how the book is received by the general audience for the niche. Goodreads has a Beta Reader group to allow authors to connect with beta readers. Some Facebook groups allow members to request beta readers. Please don't join a group just to look for beta readers. Be active in the groups. No matter how a reader is selected, do so. Give them the list of common errors (below) and ask for them to find these problems.

Mr. Mod's Checklist

Mr. Mod offers a good beginning list of items to look for during the electronic preview. Let's start there.

- **Sloppy Typography**

  This simply means font. (Merriam-Webster: the style, arrangement, or appearance of printed letters on a page.) I don't know an author who tries to double as designer who doesn't get carried away with fonts. Using something cute or scrolly, generally will have some problems. It may look good on the computer monitor previewer, but we don't know what device the reader is using or the settings. Go simple. If the words look strange in the preview, go back to see what the problem is.

- **Misspelled Words**

This should never happen, but it does. Being dependent on a spell checker is the most common reason for misspelled words, or for the wrong word being used. Not only should *you* reread and then read it again, others should look at the manuscript specifically to look for misspelled words and incorrect punctuation. One method I use is reading backward. Well, it's actually looking at the words from right to left. This forces me to look at the word rather than reading a sentence and allowing my brain to fill in what I miss.

- **Confusing Page Breaks**

Along with odd page breaks, some ways of formatting between chapters cause blank pages to show up between the chapters or before and after an image. Don't use multiple blanks lines; always use the built-in page break command in the word processor.

- **Poor Readability**

Often we think of readability as the word choice or even the reading level. With an e-book, there is also the line spacing, paragraph spacing, and how the font resizes to consider. Often different devices will show these little errors.

- **Incorrect TOC links**. What does the reader menu look like?

- **Misaligned Bullets and Number List** and formatted evenly throughout the book.

- **Broken Tables or Non-existing images**

  Tables should be rendered as images. If the images aren't displaying, then the image file wasn't included with the conversion.

End Notes

1. Mod, Craig, 2010, "How to fix today's ebook readers,"
   Gizmodo, April 22, 2010, accessed January 20, 2016, http://
   gizmodo.com/5522341/how-to-fix-todays-ebook-readers

FORMATTING CHECKLIST

☐ Save in a new file, even a new file folder.

☐ File Name. Give the manuscript a file name easily recognized by the reader. This is especially true for PDF or e-books downloaded from a website.

☐ Cover. Begin looking for a graphic artist. Begin looking at cover examples.

☐ Convert the manuscript to DOC or DOCX.

☐ Remove graphics, sidebars, and pull quotes.

☐ Remove page numbers, footnotes, and other information in header and/or footer.

☐ Remove cover image.

☐ Remove blank pages.

☐ Move endorsements, dedication, author profile, etc. to end of manuscript.

☐ Remove all formatting.

- ☐ Remove page breaks.
- ☐ Font. Use serif for body text (i.e. Times New Roman). Use sans serif for chapter titles and subheads. (i.e. Ariel).
- ☐ Add bold, underline, and italic.
- ☐ Change or add page breaks.
- ☐ Format paragraphs.
- ☐ Format chapter titles using Heading 1 style.
- ☐ Format subheads using Heading 2 style (this can be done at the same time as chapter titles).
- ☐ Create and link the table of contents.
- ☐ Add front matter.
- ☐ Link endnotes.
- ☐ Link website URLs.
- ☐ Add images, text boxes, or tables.
- ☐ Add the cover image.
- ☐ Upload to e-publisher.
- ☐ Preview the e-book.
- ☐ Correct any problems that may show up.
- ☐ PUBLISH.

To print this checklist, go to
http://bit.ly/format_checklist.

E-PUBLISHING TERMS

Aggregator – A company that distributes and sells a book to a wide range of online booksellers.

Affiliate link – A special URL for that redirects web viewers to a business website. The affiliate—the website being viewed—often receives a small commission for sales made through the affiliate link.

ASIN – Amazon Standard Identification Number. KDP assigns this number to all Kindle products.

AZW – Kindle's proprietary file for the Kindle products. It is based on the MOBI file type. The initials may stand for Amazon Word.

Backlist – A list of older books a publisher lists in the back of a catalog.

Back matter – The material in a book after the main text, such as bibliography, endnotes, or glossary.

Creative Commons License – A standardized copyright license to allow permission to share and use creative works. It is not an alternative to a copyright

Crowdfund or crowdsource – Funding a project with small amounts of money from a large number of people, usually through a service on the internet.

Digital rights management (DRM) – A system of copy protection for digital media.

E-book – An electronic book is a publication in digital form designed to be read on a computer or hand-held device. It can be a full-length book or a magazine.

EPUB – Electronic publication. An electronic file readable on a variety of devices.

Front matter – The pages of a book before the main text, such as title page, copyright page, and table of contents. It can also include endorsements and acknowledgements.

GUI – Graphic User Interface. A computer interface for users to interact with electronic devices, using graphic icons. Windows is a GUI platform.

Hyperlink – An electronic link so a reader can jump directly to a specific location in a book or on the internet.

HTML – HyperText Markup Language. Programming language that tells web pages how to render the information.

ISBN – International Standard Book Number. A thirteen-digit number assigned to products for identification within the publishing industry.

Keywords – Words used to describe a publication. These are commonly used in search features.

KDP – Kindle Direct Publishing.

Metadata – Data that provides information about other data. A visual example might be a library card catalog gives information about the books in a particular library. Metadata for an electronic publication may be the book title, subtitle, or author's name.

MOBI – An e-book file type. The term originated as the file format for the Mobipocket Reader.

PDF – Portable Document File. A file designed to be read on most computer platforms and electronic devices.

Pt – Points. A measure of length commonly used to measure the height of a font, as in "12 pt." One point is 1/72th of an inch

Px – Pixel. A single dot in an image. It is the smallest unit of digital image data.

Reflowable – An electronic document that adapts the "pages" to the settings of the device being used. A web page is a reflowable document.

Traditional publishing – Selling the rights of a manuscript to a company for printing and distribution in exchange for a percentage of the profits.

SET UP KINDLE DIRECT PUBLISHING (KDP) ACCOUNT

Setting up a KDP account is not difficult; it's a matter of answering questions.

Go to kdp.amazon.com. Sign in using your Amazon account. If you don't have an Amazon account (and what writer doesn't?), you can create one. You may want to create another Amazon account for KDP to keep your business separate from personal. I used my personal account so I won't have to remember additional log-in information.

Once signed in to the account, a page for publisher information, tax details, and royalty payments comes up. This information needs to be provided only one time.

- *Author/Publisher Information* – You may choose to select a company name or use your own name. It's beyond the scope of this book to discuss legal or tax information about setting up a company.

- *Payment & Banking* – This is the section that lets Amazon know where and how to send payments. If direct deposit is requested, bank information will be required. Direct deposit is not required. Amazon will send a check, but it will take longer to get paid.
- *Tax Information* – This is self-explanatory.

After all the information is completed, click Save in the bottom right corner.

APPENDIX 4

FORMATTING PDF E-BOOKS

A PDF e-book can look exactly like a print book. In fact, CreateSpace and other printers use complete PDF files. It's the author's preference whether to format for PDF before or after the Kindle or other e-book.

A PDF is not a flowing document as the other formats are. While it's possible to set a PDF document to reflow, it doesn't maintain the formatting well. The reader must set the reflow option. It's done by clicking on View in the top menu, Zoom, then Reflow.

There are applications specifically for reading PDF versions, such as **Adobe Reader**. Nearly all devices can read PDF files. They are easy to upload to a website or blog or send via email. I offer my books as PDF files as well as Kindle. A PDF file can be used for promotion or sent to a reviewer.

Steps to creating a PDF e-book

Format the document completely, including page numbers, headers/footers, covers, and graphics. This can be done with a word processor or a design program such as InDesign or Quarx Express. Don't create the hyperlinks to websites or bookmarks for the table of contents or index. This will be done later.

Blank Pages

If the PDF file is being created for printing, consider leaving the blank pages as used in a print book. This allows readers the ability to print two-sided and have a document that looks like a bound book. Another consideration, however, is for the reader using an e-reader. Those blank pages may become an annoyance. It's a matter of preference. It's possible to have two PDF files, one for printing and one for e-reading.

Convert the Document to PDF

Word
In the **File** menu, click on **Save As**. In the **Format** menu, select **PDF**. Then **Save**.

Open Office
In the **File** menu, click on **Export PDF**.

Pages
In the **File** menu, select **Export**, then **PDF**.

Once the document is converted to PDF, the details, such as hyperlinks and bookmarks, can be added.

Adding Navigation Details

Unless using Word 2016, these steps require Adobe Acrobat. In Word 2016, a DOC file with hyperlinks and bookmarks can be exported as a PDF file. In the **Save As** menu, select **PDF** as the file format. Choose whether the file will be printed or is for electronic distribution. For e-books, use electronic distribution.

Hyperlinks

Each hyperlink needs to be formatted individually as in other e-documents.

1. Use the **Link Tool**, found in the **Tools** menu. Click **Advanced Tools** in the drop-down menu, then **Link Tool**. This tool is also available though the link icon on the toolbar.

2. With the crosshair cursor, draw a box around the words to be linked. Don't just draw a line under the words. A box creates a link for the entire box. The reader can then click

on the word. The line option makes only a link on that line and is difficult for the user to "grab" and click.

3. A dialog box title **Create Link** will open. There are several option in that box. Make the following selections.

Link Type: Select **Visible Rectangle**.

Line Style Select **Underline**.

Highlight Style: Invert.

Line Thickness: This is a personal preference. I use thin because I like the way it looks in the final document.

Link Action: Open a web page.

Click **Next**.

Solid or Dashed may be used for Line Style; however, these selections put a complete rectangle around the words. The problem is for a nicely formatted document each rectangle needs to be the same size around the words, a crazy-making proposition during the formatting process.

1. To enter the URL in the next dialog box, I recommend using copy and paste from a web browser rather than typing. If it is a long URL, mistakes are easy to make. Click **OK**.

2. Go through the document and create all hyperlinks.

Table of Contents

Like other e-books, the table of contents needs to be linked individually. The steps aren't hard. Whether to also include subheads in the TOC is a personal preference. Generally, the direct links use the same steps as URL.

Follow the hyperlink instructions with the exception of **Link Action**. Select **Go to a page view** for this option.

A new box will open, **Create Go to View**.

The instructions in this" box are somewhat vague. Either scroll to the page that is being linked to, click on the page, then click on **Set Page**. Or use the page navigation in the toolbar to select a specific page, click on the page, then click **Set Page**.

Follow these steps for each item in the table of contents.

Index

Each page number in the index can be linked using the same method as used creating the linked table of contents. It is a nice feature for reference books and textbooks, but the task is tedious. Like other e-books, the index is being removed in favor of the search feature.

Bookmarks

PDF files also offer an option for bookmark navigation. Bookmarks are accessed through **View**, then **Navigation Panels**, and finally **Bookmarks** or with the icon on the left side of the screen.

To create bookmarks

1. Open the **Bookmark** panel.

2. Use the **Add Bookmark** tool in the **Document** dropdown menu or use the **Add Bookmark** icon at the top of the Bookmark panel. The icon is on the top right of the Bookmark panel and looks like a bookmark with a yellow star on it.

3. Navigate to the page to be bookmarked.

4. Click on the page.

5. Click on **Add Bookm**ark.

6. Double click on the bookmark in the panel on the left to change the name.

7. Bookmarks of subheads, tables, graphics, or other items can be nested under a main bookmark, such as the chapter title. Follow the instructions to bookmark the page with the page to be nested. After naming the bookmark,

highlight it and drag it on top of the main bookmark. It's possible to have several levels under a main bookmark.

Document Security

For Adobe Acrobat and Adobe Reader

1. Click on **File** then **Properties**

2. Click the **Initial View** tab

*   In **User Interface** at the bottom of the window, click **Hide Menu Bar** and **Hide Tool Bars**.
*   Or click **Open in Full Screen** mode in the **Windows Option** section.

    I like to have the **Navigation tab** in **Layout and Magnification** set for Bookmarks Panel and Page (top drop-down menu) so the navigation bookmark panel opens. So I don't use Full Screen mode.

3. Now click **Security** tab

4. In the drop-down **Security Mode** menu, select **Password Security**.

5. A **Password Security** menu will open.

6. Set **Compatibility** drop-down menu item to Adobe 5.0.

   This allows people with older Adobe Readers to open the file without problems.

7. In the **Permission Section**, click **Restrict Editing and Printing of Document**.

8. Set the password in the box.

9. Be sure to record the password so the document can be opened later for changes.

10. Set **Layout and Magnification**. If allowing printing, set the resolution.

    I set **Layout and Magnification**.

11. Set **Changes Allowed** to **None.**

12. Maintain text access for screen reader to allow for the visually impaired to use a reader to access the text.

13. Click **OK.**

    A box will pop up asking for confirmation of the password.

14. After entering the password, click **OK** again.

15. Then click **OK** one last time.

The Document Security Restrictions change isn't seen until the file has been saved and re-opened. After it has been saved and re-opened, there will be no menu bars at the top to access the **Save** functions. Because there's no menu bar, consider putting instructions at the beginning of the document about how to print using keyboard commands.

From Word

Word and other word processor programs allow limited security to be added to a PDF during the conversion or export process.

- Windows

1. Select **Save As** from the **File** menu.

2. In the **Save As Type** drop-down menu, select **PDF**.

3. Select the **Options** button.

4. Check **Encrypt the document with a password**.

5. Enter the password and click **Save**.

Word for Windows only has an option for a password to open the document. There is no option to limit editing or printing.

- Mac

1. Select **Print** from the File menu or use CMD+P.

2. In the lower left corner, use the PDF drop-down menu to select **Save as PDF**.

3. Select **Print** in the lower right corner.

4. When the **Save-As** box opens, select **Security Options** in the lower left corner.

5. Select the security options desired; hit **OK** to save the document.

Be sure to name the file to identify that it's secure and record the password.

From OpenOffice

Follow the Mac instructions.

Caution

The links created in the PDF file will not be available to readers using a Kindle or Kindle app.

CHANGES FOR EPUB FILES

Nook, iBooks, and other lesser-known e-readers use EPUB files. Generally, EPUB files are formatted the same way as Kindle files. There are enough subtle differences that it's worth the extra effort to make the necessary changes.

Conversion software is available to change a DOC, PDF, or MOBI file to an EPUB. However, the conversion process may leave a few minor, or major, formatting issues. Of course, it's possible go through the converted file and look for the problems. But it may take more hours than just preparing a DOC file for EPUB publishing in the first place.

Let's get started on the changes:

- Save the file that has already been cleaned with a new file name to indicate it is an EPUB manuscript.

- Change the chapter breaks from **Page Break** to **Section Break**. EPUB devices ignore Page Breaks and handle line spaces differently.

- Change fractions from the Word symbol for the fraction to the digits, such as "1/4." Some EPUB readers don't translate the Word symbols correctly.

- Remove superscript or subscripts. These increase the space between lines of text.

- Some EPUB readers don't recognize internal or external links. I leave them in for those that can use them.

- Use Microsoft Word's built-in bulleted list tool to create a bulleted list. Do not insert symbols to create bullets—most symbols will translate into a question mark ("?").

- Use Microsoft Word's built-in numbered list tool to create a numbered list or multilevel outline.

- Use Caps Lock to type in capital letters for text to appear in all capital letters. Do not use the Word format for all caps.

- For small caps, type in all capital letters and change the font size for the text area where small caps are to appear. Do not use the Word format for small caps.

- Do not use columns.

- To indent a large portion of text, for example when creating block quotes, use Word margin controls.

- Images should centered on the page. Click on the image and select **Wrap Text**. Set this option to **In Line with Text** so the text will be above and below the image.

Programs to help with EPUB

(This is not a tutorial for each of these programs. Just a list of what is available.)

Calibre

Calibre is a popular conversion program. This free program converts to several file formats. The formatting error messages are not clear.

Sigil

Sigil is a program to create EPUB files. The manuscript must be an EPUB, HTML, or TXT file to open in Sigil. It's more technical in the nature of formatting. However, the **Book View** can be used, which is similar to a word processor, to format. The **Flight Crew** tool points out errors. Sigil gives an option to make the corrections manually or to allow the program to automatically make corrections. For those comfortable with HTML, the HTML file can be viewed to make finer changes.

Others

Pages (Mac only), InDesign, and Scrivener are other programs to create EPUB files. Pages and Scrivener are primarily word processing programs. They do a fair job of converting simple files. InDesign is a design program. A very detailed file can be created and converted to EPUB and PDF while maintaining the formatting.

METADATA AND KEYWORDS

M etadata and keywords work together to help readers find a book in an online bookstore, as well as with search engines.

Metadata

Metadata is information about the book. When a reader searches within an online bookseller, metadata is part of the search response. It includes the author's name, publisher, book title, subtitle, description information, categories, and target audience.

Most companies ask for this information as part of the uploading process. If using a conversion program, such as Calibre, this information can be added manually. (Use the Metadata menu item and fill in the various sections. Comments can be used add a description.) When creating a PDF e-book, the metadata can be added in the Properties options. (In Adobe Reader and Acrobat, in the File drop-down menu, select Properties. In the

Description tab, fill in Title, Author, Keywords, and Description to create the metadata.)

It's important to fill in all the blanks to have as much information embedded in the metadata so the e-book will rise to the top of a search.

Keywords

Keywords are the words people use to search for a topic. In the case of a book, these words are used to find it in an online bookstore. A keyword may be a single word, such as "e-book," or a phrase, such as "formatting an e-book." Think what question a buyer might ask to find information on the topic of the book. For fiction, include genres and age groups.

Determining keywords for a book is similar to finding keywords for search engine optimization (SEO). Experts say the best combination is high search volume and low competition. One way to find this information is with Google's AdWords Keyword Planner. Although this tool is designed to determine words for Google ads, it is used widely for SEO keywords.

To use the Keyword Planner, a Google log-in is needed. If you use Google Chrome, have a Gmail account, or use another Google service, you probably have a log-in.

- Go to http://www.google.com/adwords/. After creating an account or signing in, the adwords home page will open.

- Go to the **Tools** menu. It is the wrench icon in the upper right corner. Click on **Keyword Planner.**

- Under **Find new keywords and get search volume data**, select **Search for new keywords using a phrase, website or category**.

- Enter one or more keywords in the box. Other options, including country and language, can be added.

- Click **Get Ideas**. This will open a page with a chart of ad group ideas.

- Click on the **Keyword Ideas** tab for potential keywords. The three columns to look at are Keyword, Avg. Monthly Searches, and Competition. There are also columns for Google ad costs. Competition is the number of Google advertisers using the keyword(s). The lower the competition the higher the ranking.

The following chart shows the keywords I searched and the various combinations. "Write an ebook" has a relatively high number of searches, but the competition is also high. Whereas "ebook format" has nearly as many searches, but the competition is low, therefore it's a better combination for my book. The phrase "mobi to epub converter" has the highest searches and low competition but isn't relevant to my topic.

Your product or service

format writers ebook

Get ideas   Modify search

Ad group ideas Keyword ideas			Columns ▾ 📊 ⬇ Download Add all (801)		
Keyword (by relevance)	Avg. monthly searches	Competition	Suggested bid	Ad impr. share	Add to plan
write an ebook	260	High	$4.26	-	
ebook formatting	210	Medium	$1.99	-	
make an ebook	170	Medium	$2.77	-	
ebook format	210	Low	$2.76	-	
ebook writer	140	High	$4.41	-	
word to epub converter	30	Low	$0.75	-	
making an ebook	140	Medium	$2.69	-	
mob to epub converter	320	Low	-	-	
make ebook	70	Medium	$2.54	-	

Show rows 30 ▾ 1 - 30 of 800 keywords |< ‹ › >|

Once the keywords are determined, combine them with the metadata. One important place is the title of the book. Using the top keyword in the title brings it to the top of the list. If two or more keywords are in the title, it brings it up more often. Notice I have both "formatting" and "e-book" in the title. This covers searches for "formatting" (or format, some search tools will use a portion of the word as well as the full word), searches of "ebook," and searches for "format(ing) ebooks."

PRINT BOOKS

Many e-book authors also plan to publish a print edition. Companies such as Lulu and BookBaby offer package deals for print and e-books. These have an upfront cost. Amazon offers opportunities to produce a print book without start-up costs.

CreateSpace is the print division of Amazon. Originally, it was the only way to publish a print edition within Amazon. Upon completion of a Kindle product, an option was available to go directly to CreateSpace. In 2016, Amazon began working to make it easier to publish both print books and e-books (KDP Print), so writers don't have to use two separate services. Now, instead of being directed to CreateSpace, KDP Print is offered. Authors who have print books through CreateSpace are being encouraged to move their paperbacks to KDP Print. (See Chapter 4 for more information about KDP Print.)

KDP Print is still a beta service. During 2017, as the more writers have used it, the service has begun to look more like CreateSpace.

Commentaters in the digital print world are speculating that eventually KDP Print will be merged with CreateSpace.

A PDF file is best for a print book through CreateSpace and KDP Print. The PDF needs to include headers, footers, page numbers, and all of the other items usually found in a print book. Grab a book from a shelf to see what formatting is included. This same PDF file can also be sold on a website.

RESOURCES

A list of the resources are available at
Practical Inspirations
http://practicalinspirations.com/format_resources/

Books

Amazon Kindle Publishing Guidelines (technical details needed for each Kindle device)

Building Your Book for Kindle (Windows and Mac version available)

Field Guide to Fixed Layout for E-books from Book Industry Study Group

Formatting Pages for Publishing on Amazon on CreateSpace by Chris McMullen

Free by Chris Anderson

From WORD to EBOOK by Ben Mackin

Goodreads for Authors by Michelle Campbell-Scott

How to Blog a Book by Nina Amir

Pictures on Kindle by Aaron Shepard

Smashwords Style Guide by Mark Coker
Smashwords Book Marketing Guide by Mark Coker
The Secrets to Ebook Publishing Success by Mark Coker
(These books are Smashwords Guides.)

Zen of eBook Formatting by Guido Henkel

Zen of eBook Marketing by Guido Henkel

Free online conversion services

(These only convert; they don't clean up files.)

Zamzar (multiple format options)
http://www.Zamzar.com

Nitro (Microsoft Office files to PDF)
http://www.pdftoword.com

Online Convert (various formats to EPUB)
http://ebook.online-convert.com/convert-to-epub

Calibre
http://calibre-ebook.com/

Calibre is free software to convert various file formats. Some e-book self-publishers use this program to convert their documents. I found it didn't do as complete of a job as I wanted. But it is good for getting a general feel for how the e-book will look in different formats.

E-book service companies

Bookbaby

http://www.bookbaby.com

Bookbaby charges an up-front fee, but advertises that they don't take a percentage of sales. A simple how-to guide is offered as a free download.

E-bookit

http://www.ebookit.com

Offers conversion, formatting, and distribution services.

Lulu

http://www.lulu.com/publish/ebooks/

Lulu is a well-known print-on-demand company, which has expanded into e-publishing. They have a downloadable guide. The free ePub converter still requires the simple formatting outlined in this book. Lulu will convert a file to EPUB free, but there are hosting cost and commissions. See the details at http://bit.ly/2BJMADc.

Publish Green

http://www.publishgreen.com

This company provides complete conversion services for a fee.

Smashwords

http://www.smashwords.com/

Very popular e-book conversion and distribution company. A style guide to prepare a Word file for their conversion process is available.

IngramSpark

http://www.ingramspark.com/

Provides services for e-books and print books including hardback books. Offers more distribution channels than Amazon.

Draft2Digital

https://draft2digital.com/

E-book formatting and distribution services. Draft2Digital doesn't have a store, but does have a 10% fee on books sold through the various e-bookstores.

E-book conversion services

Melinda Martin Publishing and Design Services

http://melindamartin.me

One-on-one design and self-publishing services. E-book conversion from a Word file, plus cover and interior design.

Jonlin Creative

http://www.jonlincreative.com/

Jonlin provides book design services as well as branding packages, social media images, and more.

E-book Formatting Fairies

http://marieforce.com/fairies/

The Fairies provide a wide variety of services from basic conversion to CreateSpace preparation.

iTunes Lists of Book Production and Delivery Services

https://itunespartner.apple.com/en/books/partnersearch

A list of service providers to help prepare e-books for iBooks store.

Vellum

https://vellum.pub/

Offers a formatting program free. A fee is required to convert the file for e-publishing and print books.

EPUB conversion programs

Sigil (convert to EPUB)

https://sigil-ebook.com/

EPUB Validator

http://validator.idpf.org/

eBookIt EPUB Validator

https://www.ebookit.com/tools/bp/Bo/eBookIt/epub-validator

A complimentary EPUB checker. It gives a list of errors but not how to fix them.

EPUB Checker for Mac

http://www.macupdate.com/app/mac/35031/epubchecker

Also found in the App Store (updated version)

Editing services

Christian Editors and Proofreaders Network
http://thechristianpen.com/

Christian Editor Connection
http://christianeditor.com/

Deb Haggerty | Freelance Editor
http://www.positivegrace.com/

Nicolas Nelson | Wordsmith Writing Coaches
http://www.wordsmithwritingcoaches.com

Kristen Stieffel | Writer • Editor • Mentor
http://kristenstieffel.com

John Vonhof | Writers & Authors on Fire
http://www.WritersAuthorsOnFire.com

Linda W. Yezak | Writer/Editor
http://lindayezak.com/

Darlene Catlett | Editor
https://www.love2edit.com/

Images

Free

Free Images
http://www.freeimages.com/

Morguefile
http://morguefile.com

Pixabay
https://pixabay.com

Mama Red Knight
List of free image websites
http://mamaredknight.com/images-for-your-social-media-posts-and-projects/

Paid

Dreamstime
http://www.dreamstime.com/

iStockPhoto
http://www.istockphoto.com/
Be sure to read all license information and attribution information before using even free images.

Marketing services

ClickBank
http://www.clickbank.com/

e-junkie
http://www.e-junkie.com/

List of lists

These websites have lists of various other websites to help with preparing and selling e-books.

Bookmarket – eBooks Production and Distribution
http://www.bookmarket.com/ebooks.htm
John Kremmer, author of *1,000 Ways to Market Your Book*, provides a long list of service for e-book publishing.

The Book Designer – Top Ten Resource Guides for e-Book Authors
https://www.thebookdesigner.com/2011/05/top-10-best-guides-for-e-book-authors/

Jane Friedman – How to Publish an Ebook: Resources for Authors
https://www.janefriedman.com/how-to-publish-an-ebook/

E-book conversion
http://wiki.mobileread.com/wiki/E-book_conversion

This is a long list of resource divided not just by topic, but also by platform.

Helpful websites

Creative Commons
http://www.creativecommons.org
This is the home of the Creative Commons rights and descriptions.

E-bay e-product policies
http://pages.ebay.com/help/policies/downloadable.html
Can e-books be sold on Ebay? Ebay has specific policies for selling e-products.

HTML help

EPUB eBooks Tutorial
http://www.jedisaber.com/eBooks/formatsource.shtml

W3Schools
http://www.w3schools.com/html/

HTML Dog
http://htmldog.com/guides/html/beginner/

A Simple Guide to HTML Cheat Sheet
http://www.simplehtmlguide.com/cheatsheet.php

Clean Up Your Ebook Files With HTML

http://blog.janicehardy.com/2014/08/clean-up-your-ebook-files-with-html.html

Word help

Style Basics
http://office.microsoft.com/en-us/word-help/style-basics-in-word-HA010230882.aspx

How to Use Microsoft Word Styles (tutorial)
http://www.word-tips.com/microsoft-word-styles/

Word Learning Zone – Microsoft Word: Styles (YouTube)
http://www.youtube.com/watch?v=_Xq_DVYxMOo

Password protect Microsoft office files
https://its.uark.edu/help/ta/217.php

Interesting articles

10 Formatting Tips for Nook (EPUB)
http://bentrubewriter.wordpress.com/2013/07/11/10-formatting-tips-for-the-nook-epub/

10 Things to Consider When Pricing E-books
http://thewritethought.com/blog/index.php/2011/08/27/10-things-to-consider-when-pricing-e-books/

10 Questions to Ask Before Committing to Any E-Publishing Service

http://janefriedman.com/2012/02/10/10-questions-epublishing/

Can Ebook Data Reveal New Viral Catalysts to Spur Reader Word-of-Mouth?

http://blog.smashwords.com/2012/04/can-ebook-data-reveal-new-viral.html

Checking ebooks

http://electricbookworks.com/kb/simple-ebook-operational-issues/checking-ebooks/

Comparison of e-book formats

https://en.wikipedia.org/wiki/Comparison_of_e-book_formats

Digital Rights Management and Privacy

https://epic.org/privacy/drm/

DRM

https://www.eff.org/issues/drm

eBook Quality and How to Avoid a Kindle Refund

http://www.sellbox.com/ebook-quality-and-how-to-avoid-a-kindle-refund/

How much should an ebook cost?

http://www.thedominoproject.com/?p=1986

How to become an ebook superstar

http://www.theguardian.com/books/2012/jun/06/become-an-ebook-superstar

How to self-publish an ebook

http://www.cnet.com/how-to/how-to-self-publish-an-ebook/

Marketing a self-published e-book

http://electricbookworks.com/kb/self-publishing/self-publishing-ebooks/marketing-a-self-published-ebook/

Sound effects for e-books

http://janefriedman.com/2014/06/27/create-first-booktrack-get-2000-new-readers/

Take Pride in Your eBook Formatting

http://guidohenkel.com/2010/12/take-pride-in-your-ebook-formatting/

The Pros and Cons of DRM

http://thefutureofink.com/pros-and-cons-of-drm/

The pros, cons, and future of DRM

http://www.cbc.ca/news/technology/the-pros-cons-and-future-of-drm-1.785237

CHAPTER RESOURCE LINKS

Chapter One

Project Guttenberg
http://www.gutenberg.org/

Chapter Three

The Last Perfect Father's Day
http://amzn.to/2CQtWHb

Kindle Direct Publishing
http://kdp.amazon.com

iBook FAQs
http://www.apple.com/itunes/working-itunes/sell-content/
books/book-faq.html

How to make Apple iPad and iPhone apps for ebooks (an overview of e-book apps)
http://www.sean.co.uk/a/journalism/create_apple_iphone_ipad_apps_for_ebooks.shtm

Kunaki
http://kunaki.com

Electronic Sales to Bookstores by Dean Wesley Smith
http://www.deanwesleysmith.com/think-like-a-publisher-11-electronic-sales-to-bookstores/

Amazon KDP Select Program
https://kdp.amazon.com/self-publishing/KDPSelect

"Should Self-Published Authors Take Advantage of the Kindle Select Program?" by Karin Bilich
http://smartauthorsites.com/2013/05/28/should-self-published-authors-take-advantage-of-the-kindle-select-program/

Lending for Kindle
http://bitly.com/KDP_lending

Authors: Piracy is Not Your Enemy by Thomas Umstattd
http://www.authormedia.com/authors-piracy-is-not-your-enemy/

How the Creative Commons Can Help Your Book Spread Like Crazy by Thomas Umstattd
http://www.authormedia.com/how-the-creative-commons-can-help-your-book-spread-like-crazy/

Editions at Play
https://editionsatplay.withgoogle.com/#/

Chapter Four

KDP Pricing Support
https://kdp.amazon.com/en_US/help/topic/G201551180

KDP Print
https://kdp.amazon.com/en_US/help/topic/G202059560

Kindle Jumpstart
https://kdp.amazon.com/en_US/help/topic/G202187740

Kindle Create
https://kdp.amazon.com/en_US/help/topic/
GHU4YEWXQGNLU94T

Comic Creator
https://kdp.amazon.com/en_US/help/topic/G201217140

Kindle Kids' Book Creator
https://www.amazon.com/gp/feature.html?docId=1002979921

Kindle Textbook Creator
https://www.amazon.com/gp/feature.html?docId=1002998671

X-Ray for Authors
https://kdp.amazon.com/en_US/help/topic/G202187230

Kindle Book Lending
https://www.amazon.com/gp/feature.html?docId=1000739811

Kindle Matchbook
https://www.amazon.com/gp/help/customer/display.
html?nodeId=201362970

KDP Select
https://kdp.amazon.com/en_US/help/topic/G200798990

Kindle Scout
https://kindlescout.amazon.com/

Kirkus
https://www.kirkusreviews.com/

Kindle Unlimited
https://www.amazon.com/gp/feature.html?docId=1002872331

Audible Audiobooks
https://www.audible.com/

ACX
http://www.acx.com/

Amazon Advantage
https://www.amazon.com/gp/seller-account/mm-product-page.
html?topic=200329700

Author Central
https://authorcentral.amazon.com/

Amazon Associates
https://affiliate-program.amazon.com/

Chapter Five

How to Publish and Sell Your Article on Kindle by Kate Harper
http://bit.ly/sell_articles

The Book Designers e-Book Cover Awards
http://www.thebookdesigner.com/2014/11/e-book-cover-design-awards-october-2014/

Smashwords
https://www.smashwords.com/

iBookStore requires an application and approval
https://support.apple.com/en-us/HT201183

Library of Congress
http://www.loc.com

Copyright
http://copyright.gov

ISBN
http://www.isbn.org

International ISBN Agency
https://www.isbn-international.org/

Bowker's Books in Print
http://www.bowker.com/products/Books-In--Print.html

Chapter Six

How Much Should an Ebook Cost? by Seth Godin
http://blog.bookmarket.com/2011/12/book-marketing-makeover-how-much-should.html

10 Things to Consider when Pricing E-Books by Stephen
Blake Mettee
http://www.thewritethought.com/2011/08/27/10-things-to-consider-when-pricing-e-books/

MailChimp
http://eepurl.com/bSGaFH

The Five Best Free Email Marketing Services
http://www.theworkathomewoman.com/free-email-marketing/

Hootsuite
https://hootsuite.com/

Buffer
https://buffer.com

Pay with a Tweet
http://www.paywithatweet.com

A Lawyer Who Is Also A Photography Just Deleted All Her Pinterest Boards Out Of Fear by Alyson Shontell
http://www.businessinsider.com/pinterest-copyright-issues-lawyer-2012-2

Getting Started with Pinterest by Laura Christianson
http://bloggingbistro.com/getting-started-with-pinterest/

How to Pinterest to Market Your Book by Rob Eagar
http://www.writersdigest.com/editor-blogs/there-are-no-rules/how-to-use-pinterest-to-market-your-book

Goodreads
http://www.goodreads.com

Goodreads Beta Reader Group
https://www.goodreads.com/group/show/50920-beta-reader-group

What Are Beta Readers? And Do You Need Them? By Chuck Sambuchino
http://www.writersdigest.com/editor-blogs/guide-to-literary-agents/questions-submitted-by-readers/what-are-beta-readers-and-do-you-need-them

Peer Reviews: Seek Quality in Your Beta Readers, Not Quantity by Chuck Sambuchino
http://www.writersdigest.com/editor-blogs/guide-to-literary-agents/peer-reviews-seek-quality-in-your-beta-readers-not-quantity

How to find a beta reader by Belinda Pollard
http://www.smallbluedog.com/how-to-find-a-beta-reader.html

How to Blog a Book
http://howtoblogabook.com

Blessing ND
http://www.blessingnd.com

***Not Marked* Crowdfunding Campaign**
https://www.indiegogo.com/projects/not-marked/

Smashwords Introduces Assetless Preorders
http://blog.smashwords.com/2015/06/smashwords-introduces-assetless.html

How to Choose Self-Publishing Distribution Options for Ebooks by Diana Horner
http://selfpublishingadvice.org/reaching-readers-how-to-choose-self-publishing-distribution-options/

Chapter Seven

Preschool: At What Cost? by Susan K. Stewart
http://bit.ly/preschool_cost

Chapter Eight

Nitro
http://www.pdftoword.com

Word
Convert footnotes to endnotes and vice versa
http://bitly.com/convert_footnotes

Chapter Nine

Word
Create or edit a table of contents
http://bitly.com/create_TOC

Chapter Eleven

Pictures on Kindle by Aaron Shephard
http://bit.ly/pictures_kindle

Gimp
http://www.gimp.com

Out and About at the Zoo by Jo Linsdell
http://bit.ly/out_at_zoo

Kindle Kids' Book Creator
http://bitly.com/kid_book_creator

Amazon Kindle Publishing Guidelines
http://kindlegen.s3.amazonaws.com/
AmazonKindlePublishingGuidelines.pdf

Chapter Twelve

KindleGen
http://amzn.to/1Sjcv69

Kindle Reading Apps
http://amzn.to/1oQct9Z

Proofing for Kindle by Aaron Shepard
http://www.newselfpublishing.com/ProofingKindle.html

Kindle Previewer Details
http://bit.ly/kindle_previewer

About the Author

My passion to inspire you
http://practicalinspirations.com/1263-2/#mission_statement

What is socialization?
http://practicalinspirations.com/what-is-socialization/

Practical preparedness list
http://practicalinspirations.com/practical-preparedness-list/

SUSAN K. STEWART

I'm Susan K. Stewart and **my passion is to inspire you** with practical and real-world solutions for your family.

How do I do that?

Homeschooling

My husband and I began homeschooling in 1981 and two weeks later was handed a leader's hat. Through failures and successes, I learned real-life homeschooling. Although our youngest child graduated in 2000, we didn't leave the homeschool community. I share practical ideas for teaching your children in the way God leads you.

Read "What is socialization?" at practicalinspirations.com.

Being Ready

Our family has found it practical to be ready for any unexpected situation. Two years into our homeschooling adventure, my husband lost his job. It was another two years before he found full-time work. We lived in California at the time, and were always ready in case of an earthquake. We found those preparations helped us maintain our homeschool and our sanity.

Being ready for those unexpected situations is practical and important. It doesn't have to cost a lot of money; you don't need an underground bunker full of MREs, or a hidden mountain hide out.

Read "Practical preparedness list" at practicalinspirations. com.

Writing, Editing, and Speaking

My writing career began with a handwritten and drawn neighborhood newspaper. A poem in my elementary school literary magazine was my published work. The rest is not history.

I continue to use the gifts God has given me to share the message he has given me. Writing, speaking, and editing, each one of these is a method I use to bring practical solutions to real world problems.

CONNECT WITH SUSAN

Facebook
http://www.facebook.com/susan.k.stewart
http://www.facebook.com/practicalinspirations
https://www.facebook.com/groups/Creating.eBooks
https://www.facebook.com/groups/harried.homeschoolers

Twitter
http://www.twitter.com/susan_stewart

Pinterest
http://www.pinterest.com/susankstewart

Instagram
http://www.instagram.com/susankstewart

Goodreads
https://www.goodreads.com/Susan_Stewart

LinkedIn
http://www.linkedin.com/in/susankstewart

Amazon Author Page
http://amzn.to/21Hmjte

Practical Inspirations News
http://eepurl.com/9vdS5

www.ingramcontent.com/pod-product-compliance
Lightning Source LLC
Chambersburg PA
CBHW072121020426
42334CB00018B/1666